AMERICA
the BEAUTIFUL

Also by Ben Carson, M.D.

America the Beautiful (with Candy Carson)

Take the Risk (with Gregg Lewis)

Think Big (with Cecil Murphey)

Gifted Hands (with Cecil Murphey)

The Big Picture (with Gregg Lewis)

AMERICA
the BEAUTIFUL

Rediscovering What Made This Nation Great

BEN CARSON, M.D.
with CANDY CARSON

ZONDERVAN®

ZONDERVAN.com/
AUTHORTRACKER
follow your favorite authors

ZONDERVAN

America the Beautiful
Copyright © 2012 by Ben Carson

This title is also available as a Zondervan ebook.
Visit www.zondervan.com/ebooks.

This title is also available in a Zondervan audio edition.
Visit www.zondervan.fm.

Requests for information should be addressed to:

Zondervan, *Grand Rapids, Michigan 49530*

Library of Congress Cataloging-in-Publication Data

Carson, Ben.
    America the beautiful : rediscovering what made this nation great / Ben Carson.
      p. cm.
    ISBN 978-0-310-33071-4 (hardcover)
    1. United States - Civilization. 2. Social values - United States. 3. United
States - Politics and government - 21st century. I. Title.
    E169.12.C294 2012
    973 - dc23   2011037506

Published in association with Yates & Yates, www.Yates2.com.

Cover design: Curt Diepenhorst
Cover photography: Peter Howard and janoid/Flikr
Interior design: Matthew Van Zomeren

Printed in the United States of America

12 13 14 15 16 17 18 /DCI/ 22 21 20 19 18 17 16 15 14 13 12 11 10 9 8 7 6 5 4 3 2 1

To those who have given
their time, resources, and even their lives
to create and preserve
"One nation under God, indivisible,
with liberty and justice for all."

Also to the late Patricia Modell
and to Art Modell,
who represent true American patriotism.

CONTENTS

PROLOGUE

THE UNITED STATES OF AMERICA is still the pinnacle nation in the world today. It is not, however, the first pinnacle nation to face a decline. Ancient Egypt, Greece, Rome, Great Britain, France, and Spain all enjoyed their time at the top of the world, so to speak—in many cases, for several hundred years. Then, as they began to decline, they all experienced some peculiar similarities: an inordinate emphasis on sports and entertainment, a fixation with lifestyles of the rich and famous, political corruption, and the loss of a moral compass.

One certainly sees this pattern being repeated in American society today, and if we continue to follow the course of other pinnacle nations prior to us in history, we will suffer the same fate. The question is, *can we learn from the experiences of those nations that preceded us and take corrective action, or must we inexorably follow the same self-destructive course?*

What was it about the United States of America—the child of every other nation—that was so different and so dramatically changed the world? For within only two hundred years of the founding of this nation, men were walking on the moon, creating artificial intelligence, and inventing weapons of mass destruction, among other things. In its relatively short history, America has transformed humankind's existence on earth. Among the many factors involved in our success was the conscious creation of an atmosphere conducive to innovation and hard work. People cared about their neighbors, and when some became fabulously wealthy, they were willing to share their proceeds with those less fortunate. There was a sense of community, which meant that everyone was responsible for everyone else, including the indigent. But perhaps most importantly, there was a well-defined vision for the nation.

For the first time in the world, a nation was envisioned that was "of, by, and for the people." This meant that there would be a great deal of individual, family, and community responsibility for everyone's lives, as opposed to government responsibility. This also meant that there would be unprecedented freedom to lead one's life without interference. A legitimate question for America to ask itself at this point in history is, do we still agree with the vision of the founding fathers? Or have we become much wiser than they were and therefore feel the need to adopt a different vision? Perhaps it is better to invest the government with great power and with the responsibility for taking care of all of us. We will consider both questions in this book.

If one goes back and looks at the belief system of many of our founding fathers, the faith they had in God, exemplified in both their words and deeds, is impressive. Some will argue that the United States has never been a moral nation because we engaged in slavery, and this certainly is an ugly chapter in our nation's history, one that we will also examine as we seek to understand what it is that makes America beautiful.

Unfortunately, many today have come to equate morality with political correctness, but I believe that political correctness is a very dangerous force. Many people fled to this country from other countries where dictators and oppressive governments tried to tell people what they could think and what they could say. The ability to think and speak freely was one of the major tenets upon which this nation was established, and I suspect that the founding fathers would turn over in their graves if they could see how such tenets are being violated on a regular basis today by people adhering to political correctness. If people can't freely speak their minds, conversations become muted and debate withers.

In this book, we will examine whether we can advance the great experiment that is the United States of America, perpetuating a free and prosperous nation that is "of, by, and for the people," and whether we can learn from the mistakes of our past. If we can, rather than seeing the decline that has characterized all other pinnacle nations before us, I believe our best days will still lie ahead of us.

— CHAPTER 1 —

AMERICA'S HISTORY OF REBELLING FOR CHANGE

OF ALL THE NATIONS IN THE WORLD, of all the social experiments that have been tried down through the centuries, there is no country I'd rather be a citizen of and call home than America. Where else but in this land of opportunity are people given so much freedom to pursue their dreams, with the potential to bring out the best in everyone?

I have been fortunate enough to visit forty-nine of America's fifty states, and I never cease to be amazed by the tremendous diversity one finds here—from big metropolitan cities to small countryside towns, from tropical islands to forested mountain ranges. Vast expanses of farmland produce more than enough food to feed our nation, and huge industrial areas produce airplanes, trains, cars, washing machines, and a host of other devices. The creative innovations of Silicon Valley and Seattle give us technological strength, and the great Northeastern corner of our country boasts some of the most prestigious educational institutions in the world. Add to that our ethnic and cultural diversity—one of our greatest strengths—and you begin to see how this nation's diversity enabled it to rapidly become a world power.

Does America have its flaws? Absolutely. We've certainly made our share of mistakes over the centuries and then some. But in spite of our missteps, our nation's history shows that out of our darkest periods, we have responded time and time again to work toward "liberty and justice for all." One of America's most respected legacies is indeed that of rebelling for change.

I grew up in inner-city Detroit and Boston at the tail end of one of those dark periods in America's history. Slavery had long been abolished, but widespread racism remained. The civil rights movement was on the verge of completely transforming the social landscape, but such change often comes slowly. And today, decades later, I can still pinpoint the moment when I came of age regarding racism in America.

My brother and I were playing in Franklin Park in the Roxbury section of Boston when I wandered away alone under a bridge, where a group of older white boys approached me and began calling me names.

"Hey, boy, we don't allow your kind over here," one of them said. He looked at the others. "Let's drown him in the lake." I could tell they weren't just taunting me, trying to scare me. They were serious, and I turned and ran from there faster than I had ever run before in my life. It was a shocking introduction for a little boy to the racism that ran through America at the time.

Growing up, we faced constant reminders of how we were less important than white people. Even some of those who claimed to be civil rights activists could be heard saying such things as, "He is so well educated and expresses himself so clearly that if you were talking to him on the telephone you would think he was white."

By that time, economic hardship had forced us to move to Boston, and we were living with my mother's older sister and brother-in-law in a typical tenement, where rats, roaches, gangs, and murders were all too common. One day my uncle William was giving me a haircut in the kitchen while we watched the news on television when I saw white police unleashing ferocious dogs on groups of young black people and mowing them down with powerful water hoses. Even little children were being brutalized.

Perhaps even worse than the overt racism that I witnessed on television was the systemic racism I witnessed in my own family. My aunt Jean and uncle William had two grown sons who frequently stayed with them in their dilapidated multifamily dwelling. My brother, Curtis, and I were very fond of our older cousins, who always made us laugh. But both of them were constantly in trouble with the police, which resulted in their brutal, racially motivated beatings or Uncle William having to bail them out of jail. Unfortunately, their close friends were drug dealers and gang members, many of whom were killed or died young. Ultimately both of my cousins were killed because of their association with the wrong people.

One could legitimately ask the question. Which is worse, overt racist behavior by the police, or a society that offered certain segments of its population little in the way of opportunities, increasing the likelihood of "criminal associations"? We didn't realize these friends of our cousins were dangerous for us to be around. We only knew that they joked around with us, gave us attention, and even brought us candy from time to time.

It wasn't just our inner-city neighborhood where racism flourished; I found it at school as well. During report-card-marking day in the eighth grade, for example, each student was supposed to take their report card from classroom to classroom and have their teacher place a grade in the designated spot. I was very excited because I had all *A*s, and I had only one more class to go for a clean sweep. That class was band, which was going to be an easy *A* since I was an excellent clarinetist. That last *A* would make me a shoo-in for the highest academic achievement award in eighth grade that year. I was beaming as I gave Mr. Mann my report card, but my joy quickly turned to sorrow when I saw that he had given me a grade of *C* in order to ruin my report card and my chances of receiving the highest academic award. I knew that my winning the award would have been an eye-opening experience for many people at Wilson Junior High School, since I was the only black student in the class.

Much to Mr. Mann's chagrin and to my delight, band was not considered an academic subject and did not count; therefore, I received the highest academic award after all. One of the other teachers was so upset about this that she literally chastised all the white students at the award ceremony in front of the entire school for allowing a black student to outperform them academically. The scene is depicted in the movie about my life, *Gifted Hands*, although in reality she ranted and raved a lot longer than the movie suggested. It was at least ten minutes, although it felt like longer.

In retrospect, I realize that all of these teachers and some of the students were simply products of their environment, but they triggered in me a strong desire to start my own personal civil rights movement to show everyone that I was just as good as they were by doing better than they did in school. As my academic awards and accomplishments continued to pile up, I had to combat feelings of superiority, which proved to be just as difficult as the task of fighting off an inferiority complex. Nevertheless, by the time I was in high school I had come to understand that people are people, and that their external appearance was not a good predictor of what kind of people they were.

In April of 1968, on the day after Dr. Martin Luther King Jr. was assassinated, a major riot broke out at my high school in inner-city Detroit. Most of the black students were so outraged that they were trying to physically harm anyone who was white. Some very serious beatings took place, and I saw many of my white friends being harassed. The student population of the school was about 70 percent black, so the white students did not have much of a chance. At the time, I held a job as the biology laboratory assistant setting up experiments for the other students. The department even trusted me with a key to the science classrooms and the greenhouse. So during the riot, I used that key to open the greenhouse and hide several white students during the melee.

By that time in my life, I understood the extent of racism in America, but I also was beginning to have hope for the future. Having lived and studied among both black and white cultures, I knew that there are good white and black people and there are bad white and black people. It mattered not what color your skin was on the outside, but rather what the condition was of your heart and mind inside. And as I better understood human nature, I felt more emboldened to do things differently than everybody else and to chart my own course for a successful life.

I think that many of the people involved in the founding of our nation also felt they were victims of injustice, but they too had a profound understanding of human nature and set out to design a system different from previous governments that would level the playing field.

Today our nation faces a challenge of a different kind—one that nevertheless requires of us all a movement to stand up for our civil rights. One that asks us to educate ourselves as to the founders' original vision for our nation and to take action to assure we protect and pursue that vision. While many nations lean on their past to give them a sense of accomplishment, the United States has a history of redefining itself and moving forward to ensure that there is indeed liberty and justice for all.

A NEW WORLD SPRINGS FORTH

The dangers that face our nation today are every bit as great as those we have faced in the past. The question is whether we have lost our capacity to endure hardship and sacrifice for future generations. We face a national budgetary crisis that threatens to rip our country apart and destroy our way of life, yet many concern themselves only with the governmental benefits they might lose. I write with the hope that we can reawaken the spirit of greatness that created the wealthiest, most compassionate, freest nation the world has ever seen. In this book we will embark upon a brief review of pertinent parts of our history that have everything to do with finding our way forward to a prosperous future.

Whether the first people to arrive on the North American continent were migratory tribes that traveled across a land bridge between what is currently Russia and Alaska, or whether they were ancient sailors who navigated the ocean — America has always had a rich and diverse ethnic background. Our nation began that way and we continue to expand that way. All kinds of people are responsible for our nation's rapid development and great accomplishments, and by the same token, we share blame for many of the atrocities that have occurred on American soil.

The impetus for Europeans to quickly settle the Americas came from the discovery of vast mineral deposits and other natural resources that could create enormous wealth. It was Amerigo Vespucci, an acquaintance of Columbus, who is credited with America's discovery in 1497, five years after Columbus landed in the Caribbean Islands while searching for a new route to the spice-rich Far East. Chinese Admiral Cheng Ho, who visited the Americas in 1421, could lay claim as well — and there is also evidence that Scandinavian explorer Leif Erikson reached the Americas hundreds of years before any of these other explorers. Regardless of who "discovered" America, Columbus's expeditions certainly raised awareness back in the Old World as to the New World's vast potential for increasing the wealth of those nations that were able to exploit it. And once this became known in the Old World countries, explorers began to arrive.

The Spaniards had significant colonies and exploited the mineral wealth here, and America could easily have been a Spanish-speaking nation, but an intense rivalry between Spain and England, particularly during the latter part of the sixteenth century, put America up for grabs. Spain's domination of the oceans was challenged by England and the Dutch, who were building an extremely large merchant marine fleet in Europe. The final nail in the coffin of Spanish domination of the oceans took place in 1588, when the Spanish Armada was sunk in a battle with the English and, more importantly, by a ferocious storm, which decimated their mighty fleet. Because the English dominated the seas in the early 1600s, they decided it was their right to begin colonizing America, and the first of the permanent English colonies, Jamestown, was established in 1607.

I still remember the idyllic pictures of the Jamestown settlement in my school books as a child, but in reality the settlement was anything but ideal. Many of the settlers were English gentlemen who had no idea how to work in a wild environment. They quickly ran out of food while battling the Algonquin and enduring very harsh winter conditions. You don't have to have much of an imagination to visualize how desperate those early settlers must have been. The vast majority of the early settlers succumbed to starvation and violence, and there are even credible reports of cannibalism. They suffered extreme hardship and personal sacrifice, all to create a more stable and prosperous future for subsequent generations.

The Europeans had also not anticipated the fierce resistance shown by the Native Americans, who had no intention of simply handing over their land. Although many movies portray the Europeans as vastly superior to the Native Americans in warfare, their most effective weapons were the diseases they brought, against which the Native Americans had no immunological resistance. These diseases wiped out whole villages and tribes through massive epidemics that were far more effective than any fighting force. While the Native Americans were being vanquished, the English, French, and Spaniards, among others, fought for the dominant position in the New World. The Jamestown colony would never have survived if it had not been for the friendship developed with the tribe of Powhatan, who taught them some basic fundamentals of farming and traded food for beads—a gracious, saving exception to the conflict and warfare that characterized our nation's early history.

In time, the English Jamestown settlement grew and thrived, especially after the introduction of indentured servants and slaves in 1619 and the development of American tobacco, which quickly became all the rage in England and other parts of Europe. The rapid growth of the tobacco industry turned out to be a financial bonanza for the fledgling colony, enabling it to survive. There were early attempts at remote self-rule, the most permanent of which was the establishment of the House of Burgess, which consisted of a governor and "councilors," appointed by the governor, and some representatives of estates.

Around the time of the establishment of the House of Burgess, a second permanent colony was being established by the pilgrims in Plymouth, Massachusetts, in the harbor of Cape Cod Bay. These religious separatists were interested in the New World primarily because they felt that their freedoms were compromised both in terms of religion and life in general. In an attempt at self-rule, they constructed an agreement of behavior known as the Mayflower Compact, the first formal constitution in North America. In this contract, they agreed to the fair and equal treatment of everyone for the good of the colony. Unfortunately, "everyone" did not include women, those who were not land owners, slaves and indentured servants, or the region's natives. To their credit, they were attempting to build a type of society that was foreign to most of the world, since most colonies were governed according to the wishes of the ruler. These were immature baby steps toward a more noble goal, but at least they were steps in the right direction.

Over the next few decades, an explosion of colonization occurred, largely from people seeking religious freedom and/or financial opportunities. Many in Europe saw an opportunity to escape the oppressive and overbearing governmental systems under which they languished, and these people emigrated in droves, bringing with them a strong determination to make a better life for themselves and their offspring, unfettered by oppressive overseers disguised as government. The opportunities to enrich themselves through their own efforts brought out the best in many people, but it also brought out avarice, greed, and a host of unethical behaviors that invariably accompany freedom. Fortunately, those whose characters were constrained by religious principles far outnumbered those lacking moral rectitude. The British remained technically in charge of all these colonies, but due to the independent-minded nature of many of the colonists and the distance involved, British control was somewhat tenuous. The other great power of Europe, France, was also vying for control and power in the New World, but they were largely distracted by their ongoing wars with the Iroquois, and seemed to be much more interested in trading and exploration than they were in establishing permanent settlements.

Throughout the mid- and late seventeenth century, immigrants flooded in not only from England, but also from France, Germany, and other parts of Europe. Migrating into the area that was to become Pennsylvania, a large influx of Quakers provided a solid base for the abolitionist movement that was to come. By the end of the seventeenth century, the colonies had become more sophisticated and organized, establishing Virginia, Massachusetts, New York, Maryland, Rhode Island, Connecticut, Delaware, New Hampshire, North Carolina, South Carolina, New Jersey, and Pennsylvania, with Georgia added in 1732. Thus the basis of the original thirteen colonies was in place.

During the rapid expansion of colonial life in America, England jealously guarded its sovereignty over America. The myth of royal supremacy engendered a royal entitlement belief known as "the divine right of kings" given by God to rule over the people. This right was ferociously guarded, and when it was challenged by British people like Colonel Algernon Sidney, public execution quickly followed. The English crown not only felt that it had a right to rule the colonies, but also to extract money from them. For several decades, England had been involved in ongoing warfare, mostly with France and Spain, which had drained the treasury; therefore, the king felt that the massive expenditures to protect the American colonies during the French and Indian War should be repaid in part by those who benefitted— namely, the colonists.

This ambitious taxation was a haunting echo of the life the colonists had experienced in the Old World and set out for the New World to escape. But it was also a harbinger of the times we find ourselves in today in America. In both instances, unrest began to stir in the people.

GROWING RESENTMENT OVER OUT-OF-CONTROL TAXATION

The British Parliament had imposed many taxes on the colonists under the revenue acts, but still they were not satisfied with the amount of money being collected. So in 1765, the Stamp Act was passed, which imposed a levy on just about every type of legal document imaginable, including mar- riage licenses, college degrees—even such ordinary items as newspapers and playing cards. Needless to say, the colonists were not pleased about this, even though British citizens in England were already paying not only this tax, but many other exorbitant taxes. The Americans felt that once they acquiesced to more British taxation, there would never be an end to escalating tax rates, so they began to boycott British products. The colonists vigorously—and sometimes even brutally—encouraged their fellow Americans to use only products produced in the New World, and they began attacking British tax collectors, sometimes beating them, or even worse, tarring and feathering them. They also used these same intimidation tactics later on fellow Ameri- cans to assure compliance with boycotts of British goods. Finally, in 1766, the British Parliament repealed many of the taxes, including the Stamp Act. The colonists celebrated the repeal, even erecting a statue of King George in New York.

It wasn't long, however, before the taxation monster raised its ugly head again, for in 1767, the Townshend Act was passed. This famously included taxes on tea, which the colonists had grown increasingly very fond of. Through trickery and parliamentary procedures, the Townshend Act allowed the British's almost bankrupt East India Company to gain a virtual monopoly on tea sales, exacerbating tensions between the colonies and Eng- land. The colonists once again decided to boycott English imports, prompt- ing an angry response from England, who sent four thousand British troops to quell the colonial protests. To sustain themselves in the New World, the British troops competed with the locals for jobs, which further inflamed tensions between the sides.

In December of 1773, some of the colonists were so outraged with the taxes on tea that they disguised themselves as Native Americans, boarded British ships in Boston Harbor, and destroyed the tea by tossing it all into the harbor. This, of course, was the famous Boston Tea Party. The British were so outraged that they closed Boston Harbor and instilled a harsher governing structure. More taxes and regulations followed, many of which were quite punitive and became known by the colonists as the "Intolerable Acts." There were frequent clashes between the locals and the soldiers without bloodshed, but this changed on March 5, 1770, when a crowd surrounded a group of redcoats in an angry confrontation and the British soldiers fired shots into the crowd. Five of the locals were killed, the first of whom was Crispus Attucks, an African-American and the first American to die in the Revolutionary War.

The tensions between Great Britain and America continued to build and numerous skirmishes, some of which are well documented by historians, broke out. One of the most famous fights took place on June 17, 1775, at Breed's Hill,[1] where approximately 2,500 British troops attacked an American installation defended by only about 1,400 troops. It was an intense battle and the British lost approximately 40 percent of their troops, while the Americans lost less than a third of theirs. Even though the British eventually won that battle, it was a Pyrrhic victory, with the devastating psychological impact of their heavy casualties impacting the rest of the war.

The combination of heavy taxation, excessive regulations, and lack of representation in their governing structures irritated the colonists to the point that many of them began talking not only about ways to protest, but also about the desire to declare independence once and for all from the British Crown. With all of their backbreaking hard work, they felt it unfair to have such a significant portion of the fruits of their labors confiscated by a government that neither represented their interests nor respected their freedom. Nevertheless, many colonists (known as Tories or Loyalists) remained loyal to the British Crown and felt that the benefits of British citizenship—or at least of being a British colony—were too great to sacrifice for an uncertain future of independence.

WAKING UP TO SOME "COMMON SENSE"

In 1776, as Washington's ragtag army kept British forces engaged, public sentiment was growing in favor of independence. All the colonists needed was a spokesman to galvanize public opinion toward resistance from Great Britain—and an unlikely figure emerged in the form of Thomas Paine. He had only been in the country for a little over a year, "arriving as a failure in almost everything he attempted in life. He wrecked his first marriage, and his second wife paid him to leave. He destroyed two businesses and flopped as a tax collector. But Paine had fire in his blood and defiance in his pen,"[2] and America was and still is a country of fresh starts.

An editor of a Philadelphia magazine, Paine published a fifty-page political pamphlet, *Common Sense*, in January of 1776, which began with one of the most memorable lines in American history: "These are the times that try men's souls." The pamphlet resonated so well with the colonists' feelings about independence that over 120,000 copies of the pamphlet were sold within the first three months, and half a million copies were sold in the first year. To put the impact of Paine's pamphlet *Common Sense* into perspective, in the United States today you would have to sell about 65 to 70 million copies of a publication — or about one copy per four to five people — to equal the proportionate distribution.

Spurred on by the message of *Common Sense*, enthusiasm for independence grew dramatically, even among former Loyalists. Paine donated the profits from the sale of *Common Sense* to George Washington's army, saying, "As my wish was to serve an oppressed people, and assist in a just and good cause, I conceived that the honor of it would be promoted by my declining to make even the usual profits of an author."[3] Thomas Jefferson even included a portion of *Common Sense* as the prelude to the Declaration of Independence, which was adopted by Congress in July of that year. The publication clearly resonated deeply with the American colonists' desire for independence.

In fact, their longing for self-government and willingness to fight — even die — for freedom became so strong that the words of politician Patrick Henry became a rallying cry for the colonists when he said, "Is life so dear, or peace so sweet, as to be purchased at the price of chains and slavery? Forbid it, Almighty God! I know not what course others may take; but as for me, give me liberty, or give me death!" Finally, in 1776, each of the colonies (except Georgia) sent delegates to the First Continental Congress, where the process began for the drafting of the Declaration of Independence.

TEA PARTIES — THEN AND NOW

The rebellion of the Boston Tea Party has many similarities with the political movement today known as the Tea Party. For the sake of simplicity, let's call the colonial protesters the old Tea Party movement and call the political movement established in 2009 the new Tea Party movement.

In the days of the old Tea Party, the British government and American Loyalists attempted to establish and maintain control of the colonies. When the Patriots first began to resist such efforts, those in power tended to deny that there was any real resistance from anyone except extremist, fringe individuals. Let's call this the *denial phase*. But as the protests became more prolific, denial was no longer tenable, and the powers that be decided to ignore the movement. Their hope was that if they paid no attention to the protesters, it would be less likely that others would join them and the movement would simply fade away. Let's call this the *ignore phase*. Unfortunately for those in control, ignoring the movement did nothing to lessen its intensity and, in fact, gave it time to grow even more powerful. The colonists ended up inflicting significant damage on those in power, forcing them to fight back, in many cases, with more force than necessary. Many of the regulations subsequently imposed were a part of this punitive *resistance phase*. The more the established powers resisted, however, the more determined the colonists were to overcome that resistance. Some of the British military leaders actually began to admire the tenacity and bravery of the colonial fighters.

After the Battle of Breed's Hill, some of the enthusiasm of the British and American Loyalists began to wane, and doubts began to creep into their thinking about whether the growing war was really one worth fighting. The British had a long and successful history of colonizing many parts of the world, which had brought them great power and wealth, but America and the Americans were different than any of the other groups they had ruled. Perhaps, they considered, America should be exempt from the sovereign dictates of the throne. Maybe they were more like England than any of the other colonies in the world.

At some point in the struggle to regain power, it becomes easier for a ruler to exempt an unruly but powerful subject from punishment than to suffer defeat. During this *exemption phase*, it became increasingly easy for the Loyalists to desert the throne and align themselves with the Patriots, who were gaining power and the admiration of the populace. Many of those formerly in power—the American Loyalists, dedicated to the British crown, for example—began to believe and act on the very things they once railed against, conforming to the ideology and actions of their previous enemies. This we shall call the *conforming phase*. The final phase is the *transformation phase*, in which the ideology of the resistance movement becomes the mainstream philosophy governing a now changed society. And in the case of the American Revolution, the ideas of the old Tea Party—less central government, more local rule, and more personal responsibility — became the basis for a new society that rapidly rose to the pinnacle of the world.

The New Tea Party: **DIRECT**ing America Today

The old Tea Party would probably have never been birthed if large segments of the colonial population had not felt oppressed and betrayed by the very government that was supposed to be taking care of their needs. If one were to make an acrostic of the first letters of each of these phases — denial, ignore, resistance, exempt, conforming, and transformation — one gets the word *DIRECT,* and that's basically what happened: an enthusiastic group of fervent believers was able to *direct* a fledgling new nation away from corrupt, oppressive, nonrepresentative government to a fairer, limited, and representative government.

Now let's look at the same *DIRECT* acrostic with respect to the new Tea Party. Late in 2008 and early in 2009, a number of things happened that caused great concern to a large number of Americans. Among these were the passage of the Emergency Economic Stabilization Act of 2008, the American Recovery and Reinvestment Act of 2009, the bailout of several major financial agencies, and talk about dramatic reform of the nation's health care system. Scattered small protests about these things were seen around the nation, but the entrenched powers of government and most of the media denied their significance.

Then on February 19, 2009, a business news editor on CNBC by the name of Rick Santelli in a national broadcast from the floor of the Chicago Mercantile Exchange severely criticized government plans to refinance "underwater mortgages," those mortgages whose values are less than the balance owed because of the collapse in housing prices. Many of the derivative traders on the floor in the background applauded, and the hosts of the show were bewildered.

The video of Santelli's outburst went viral, with special emphasis on the part where he called for another tea party, during which traders would gather all of the derivatives for their mortgages and dump them in the Chicago River in protest of the massive corporate infusion at the expense of taxpayers. Shortly after that, many people on television began to refer to the various local protests as "tea parties." The entrenched political establishment and most of the media ignored how fast these protests were growing, just as the British had regarded the colonial protests during the American Revolution. However, as the numbers and intensity of these protests began to multiply, the media began to make fun of the protesters in the hope that this would discourage others from joining in. The passage of the new health care legislation in December of 2009, contrary to what the majority of Americans wanted, was like pouring gasoline on a fire, and it dramatically increased the strength of the Tea Party movement. From the perspective of those in the new Tea Party, not only was the government spending money that it didn't have at an alarming rate, but it had now enacted a gigantic federal program that was going to be very expensive and impose freedom-robbing regulations.

As the protests grew, however, they could no longer be ignored, and the resistance phase began to set in. The attacks from much of the media, from several members of Obama's administration, and from the Democratic Party were relentless and mean-spirited. As with the colonial Tea Party, resistance only served to strengthen the movement, which was beginning to be joined by many notable political figures and other individuals. During the 2010 midterm primaries, Tea Party membership had grown to the point that it was able to significantly influence the outcome of the primaries. Since their values were more closely aligned with the values of the Republican Party than those of the Democratic Party, they concentrated on the Republican primaries, where they prevailed in several states, removing the entrenched traditional Republican candidate and replacing them with a Tea Party candidate.

It became increasingly clear that the Tea Party was not simply an arm of the Republican Party, but rather a significant force for real change. Its constituents recognized that both the Democrats and the Republicans were responsible for excessive spending, incessant pork barrel projects to benefit special constituent groups, and intrusion into the private lives of citizens. Tea Party members were especially outraged by the fact that the president and Democratic congressional leaders did not seem particularly interested in the feelings of the people, as manifested by their cramming of the health-care bill down the throats of the American people. As with the colonial Tea Party, denial, ignoring, and resistance had all failed to stem the tide; therefore, it was time for them to exempt themselves from the struggle to quash the rebellion.

Commentators stopped deriding the Tea Party and began recognizing it as a legitimate political force. They began to think that maybe it was different from some of the other fringe movements that had popped up over the course of the preceding decades. Officials of the Obama administration stopped calling them "tea baggers" and began treating them with respect. As this book is being written, the conforming phase is beginning, and I wouldn't be surprised to see the transformation phase arise before or soon after the 2012 presidential election.

OUR NATION IS IN HOT WATER

For several decades now, America has basically had a two-party system: Democrats and Republicans. Each of these parties has been engaged in the gradual but consistent growth of the central government and its claim on power. Ever-expanding programs offering benefits to the masses are difficult to resist, and with the proliferation of the news media it also became possible for elected officials to gain great notoriety and power. This power became addicting to many elected officials who, instead of going to Washington, DC, for a brief time to represent their constituency, wanted to hold their positions for extended periods of time—even for life. This growing power and the progressive intrusion of government into the lives of the people was so insidious that it went largely undetected. This process is much like the frog that willingly sits in the saucepan as the temperature is gradually increased until the water is boiling, killing the frog. The frog would have immediately jumped out of the saucepan, however, if the water was already boiling from the beginning.

In early 2009, many throughout America voiced their discontent as they began to worry about the excessive government spending for such programs as TARP (Troubled Assets Relief Program) and the proposed bailout for many Wall Street entities and large companies such as General Motors. The country was already in significant debt, with no clear indication of how that money was going to be repaid. It is easy to see how our growing debt, excessive spending, and elected leaders ignoring the will of the people closely resembles the set of circumstances that precipitated the American Revolution.

WILL WE ONCE AGAIN REBEL FOR POSITIVE CHANGE?

America got off to an auspicious start centuries ago because its citizens were unwilling to be herded like sheep by an elite group of "leaders." They were driven instead by a desire to take ownership of their own fate and establish a nation created by them and for them. Their self-determination and celebration of freedom to control their own lives helped birth our great nation.

Today, however, a fundamental shift has occurred in the role of our nation's government and the role of its people, and so throughout this book, we will determine whether those seeds of independence still remain viable or whether they have been supplanted by passivity and acceptance of the status quo. For freedom is an elusive bird, constantly on the move, progressively distancing itself from complacency. Do we value our freedom enough to pursue it, or have we lost our way without realizing it? Do we benefit from the principles that established this nation without understanding them?

What will we as America's citizens write in this next chapter of our history? Will we settle for being herded by our leaders' understanding of what is best for us? Or will "we the people" once again rally together, educating ourselves as to the best possible solutions for a way forward, communicating to our leaders our collective desires, and demonstrating that we truly are a nation that rebels for positive change?

—CHAPTER 2—

WHO ARE "WE THE PEOPLE"?

GROWING UP, MY BROTHER, Curtis, and I frequently disagreed about who was responsible for the chaos in the cramped bedroom we shared. We often left our clothes strewn about and our beds unmade, and the boundary dividing our room into his half and mine shifted depending on how much of our stuff was lying around and which one of us was having friends over.

Father was no longer at home to provide any leadership. He had left the family when Mother found out he had been living as a bigamist across town. Mother wasn't home much, either—but for very different reasons. She was almost always out working, trying to provide for us as best she could. Consequently, we almost never had anyone around the house to referee our disputes or hound us to do our chores.

How was Mother able to establish effective rules in such a chaotic situation? Although we got into a fair amount of trouble at home, there never were any serious incidents because we had guidelines that governed our behavior in the absence of an authority figure. Mother was smart enough to realize that if she simply imposed rules on us, we were unlikely to follow them; therefore, she involved us in the rule making. We all had a say in who would do the dishes, who would sweep the floors, who would warm the food, who would take out the garbage, and so on. We also agreed upon the punishment for not carrying out one's duties and the rewards for doing a stellar job. This system of governance was well defined and well accepted, so there was almost no trouble. I am frequently asked why Curtis and I obeyed our mother when sometimes we didn't see her for an entire week. The answer is quite simple—they were not just *her* rules, they were also *our* rules, for ownership of an idea makes cooperation with its tenets much more likely.

So Curtis and I had to come to solutions ourselves regarding our room, and that is exactly what we did. In order to make things work, we simply each accepted responsibility for the entire room for a week at a time. The room was cleaner than ever because it was always clear where responsibility lay.

We were part of the family, and Mother treated us that way. She didn't coddle us or tell us what to do every step of the way, as if we were incapable of making decisions on our own. She wanted us to contribute to the success of our family as a prelude to becoming successful in the world.

OWNERSHIP OF AN IDEA LEADS TO GREATER COOPERATION

Throughout history, we humans have attempted to create rules that would lead to peace and prosperity, as well as fairness among the nations. Unfortunately, those goals have rarely been achieved, despite numerous and varied attempts throughout time and around the world. If we have learned over the centuries and have become so smart, why is it so difficult for us to make progress in these areas? If ownership of an idea makes cooperation with its tenets much more likely, why can't the same principles work for a larger society?

The fact of the matter is, there are many examples in early American history where self-governance did work—and extremely well at that. Many of the Quaker societies and the Amish and Mennonite communities functioned efficiently, peacefully, and fairly. Perhaps the past tense is not the best one to use, since many of the Amish and Mennonite communities are still thriving today. We see many patients from these communities at Johns Hopkins Hospital, and we are always thrilled to admit them because they are very friendly and extremely cooperative. They pay their bills and you never have to worry about them trying to sue you. If everyone were that way, medicine would be a much more pleasant profession and costs would be considerably lower. There are no homeless people in these communities and extremely little crime. Among them, there is a strong sense of caring for one's neighbor, yet hard work on the individual level is still rewarded. Many people in these communities own businesses and have accumulated substantial wealth, which is beneficial to everyone else in the community since many jobs are created as businesses expand in a free environment.

Many nations, such as ancient Israel and the medieval English, made admirable attempts at establishing fair and peaceful societies. Their principal idea was to allow the people to govern themselves as much as possible.

Ancient Israeli government, for example, was set up as a commonwealth of freemen. "Proclaim liberty throughout all the land unto all the inhabitants thereof," reads Leviticus 25:10, in celebration of the Year of Jubilee. Their basic belief was that all men should be free, and the founding fathers of our nation echoed that belief by having this same verse inscribed on the Liberty Bell. The people of ancient Israel were organized into small groups of families, and each of those families had a voice and vote in that group through a representative. Representatives of those groups reported to a higher-level group, and this continued until you reached the topmost governing level. Strong, local government to solve problems on the level at which they occurred kept the number of cases that rose to the highest level to a manageable number. ("The hard causes they brought unto Moses," reads Exodus 18:26, "but every small matter they judged themselves.") They focused on reparation to the victim rather than punishment or fines levied on the perpetrator, and common consent of the people was necessary for new laws and elections (or rejections) of leaders.[1] The accused were presumed innocent until evidence revealed beyond a shadow of a doubt their guilt. In rare, borderline cases, the decision was made in favor of the accused with the mind-set that if he had actually committed the crime, that punishment could be left to God in the afterlife.

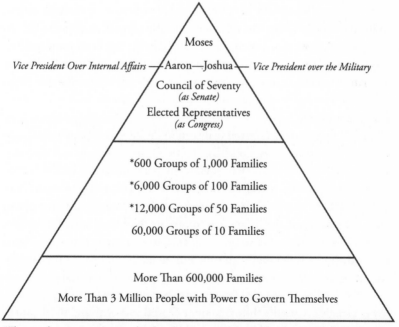

Moses

Vice President Over Internal Affairs —Aaron—Joshua— Vice President over the Military

Council of Seventy
(as Senate)

Elected Representatives
(as Congress)

*600 Groups of 1,000 Families

*6,000 Groups of 100 Families

*12,000 Groups of 50 Families

60,000 Groups of 10 Families

More Than 600,000 Families

More Than 3 Million People with Power to Govern Themselves

*These numbers are approximations based on the census recorded in the first chapter of the book of Numbers

In Anglo-Saxon Common Law, as in the Israeli setup, the people were a commonwealth of freemen. Every adult had a voice and vote, and the groups of families were organized in units of ten, each with an elected leader. Like the Israelis, those leaders had representatives from their groups that met on a higher level, and attempts were always made to solve problems on the level where the problem originated. It was systems such as these that inspired our nation's founding fathers to promote not only cooperation, but widespread participation.[2]

DEMOCRACY WAS NEVER INTENDED AS A SPECTATOR SPORT

The founding fathers of America were extremely well-educated men and great students of history, "the well fed, well bred, well read, and well wed," as historian James McGregor Burns described them.[3] They represented a nouveau aristocracy, not by birth as in the mother countries, but through development of their minds and talents.

These men certainly feared having a government that was too big and too powerful, as they had experienced across the ocean, so when trying to assemble an appropriate governing structure for this country, these dedicated Americans deliberated for over four weeks trying to decide what kind of government we would have. This included heated philosophical and political discussions over the tenets of Aristotle's six forms of political constitution, ranging from tyranny and monarchy to democracy and polity.[4] The situation was too critical for them to leave the organization of the new government to just anyone, and so they ultimately incorporated many of the best ideas from other cultures along with a heavy dose of faith in God and a lot of hard work.

Could a government's power truly rest in the hands of the people? Could such an experiment really work? By definition, in legislative- and decision-making processes, a democracy requires full participation of all the people. But most people are so involved and preoccupied with daily duties and routines, they have neither the time nor energy to participate in hearings and study the issues sufficiently enough to prepare for a vote. Several times the ancient Greeks attempted to utilize democratic mass participation in governing their city-states, but each time it resulted in tyranny. As the population expands, a democracy becomes increasingly inefficient and rowdy.

Although the noble goal of democracy had been tried by other societies, power usually eventually shifted to some central authority and the dream of autonomy died. Even with the well-established system of democracy created by the ancient Israelis, the people became dissatisfied and demanded a king. Without question, when one has a central authority figure the squabbling and arguments quickly die out and it is easier to get things done. The founding fathers understood this tendency and endeavored to create a system that would resist the urge to become a monarchy. Yes, there had been benevolent kings and queens, but they had experienced firsthand a monarch who cared not for the populace at large.

This process of developing a government that could utilize the power bestowed on it by the people to govern effectively but efficiently was tricky business. These men had witnessed the tyranny of monarchs and the ineffectiveness and inequality of large governments, and they recognized that a democracy would quickly stagnate if everybody had to weigh in on every decision. Therefore, they decided that a republic-type government would be much more efficient, in which elected representatives of the people would make decisions. Also, with a republic there is no limitation on expansion.

"A republic, by which I mean a government in which the scheme of representation takes place," stated James Madison in *The Federalist Papers*, "opens a different prospect and promises the cure for which we are seeking."[5] A republic, he further defined, is "a government which derives all its powers directly or indirectly from the great body of the people, and is administered by persons holding their offices during pleasure for a limited period, or during good behavior. It is *essential* to such a government that it be derived from the great body of the society, not from an inconsiderable proportion or a favored class of it; otherwise a handful of tyrannical nobles, exercising their oppressions by a delegation of their powers, might aspire to the rank of republicans and claim for their government the honorable title of republic."[6]

In other words, if this new government was to survive and flourish down through the centuries, it would need a way to prevent the abuse of power.

THE CHECKS AND BALANCES, PLEASE

At the Constitutional Convention, where the US Constitution was drafted, the founders decided to divide power within the federal government to ensure that it would not be controlled by just one man or one group. Three divisions or branches were the result: the executive branch, the legislative branch, and the judicial branch, each of which has duties concerning the law.

The job of the legislative branch, which consists of the House of Representatives and the Senate, is to create laws when necessary—and there was never any intention that they would just sit around arbitrarily creating laws, particularly laws that benefitted special interest groups. The executive branch, which includes the president, the vice president, the office of the attorney general, and the departments governed by each of the cabinet secretaries, all execute the laws provided by the legislative branch. All cabinet-level appointments were to be confirmed by the Senate, and there was no provision for the appointment of czars—as we have today to oversee the implementation of policies ranging from the recovery of the US auto industry to the doling out of economic stimulus—without official oversight. Finally, the judicial branch interprets the laws. In recent decades, however, we have seen more activism by the judicial branch, which is why there is so much bickering surrounding each nomination to the Supreme Court. Each and every political persuasion wants someone appointed who is philosophically aligned with them, with the hope that the judge's activism will work in their favor. Again this was not the original intention of the founding fathers, and it is a good reason why we need to consider term limits for Supreme Court Justices.

Each of the three branches has the ability to impact the activities of the other two, creating a system of checks and balances. This was an ingenious system created by our founders to help avoid the kinds of tyrannical governmental systems from which they had fled. As long as we maintain a degree of balance in the three branches of our government, we are unlikely to tilt too far in one direction or the other, thereby destroying our democracy. "In framing a government which is to be administered by men over men," James Madison pointed out, "the great difficulty lies in this: you must first enable the government to control the governed; and in the next place, oblige it to control itself."[7]

BASIC POWERS AND CHECKS

EXECUTIVE POWERS (PRESIDENT)
- Approves or vetoes federal bills.
- Carries out federal laws.
- Appoints judges and other high officials.
- Makes foreign treaties.
- Can grant pardons and reprieves to federal offenders.
- Acts as commander-in-chief of armed forces.

CHECKS ON EXECUTIVE POWERS
- Congress can override vetoes by 2/3 vote.
- Senate can refuse to confirm appointments or ratify treaties.

- Congress can impeach and remove the president.
- Congress can declare war.
- Supreme Court can declare executive acts unconstitutional.

LEGISLATIVE POWERS (CONGRESS)

- Passes federal laws.
- Establishes lower federal courts and the number of federal judges.
- Can override the president's veto with 2/3 vote.

CHECKS ON LEGISLATIVE POWERS

- Presidential veto of federal bills.
- Supreme Court can rule laws unconstitutional.
- Both houses of Congress must vote to pass laws, checking power within the legislature.

JUDICIAL POWERS (SUPREME COURT)

- Interprets and applies the law by trying federal cases.
- Can declare laws passed by Congress and executive actions unconstitutional.

CHECKS ON JUDICIAL POWERS

- Congress can propose constitutional amendments to overturn judicial decisions. (These require 2/3 majority in both houses, and ratification by 3/4 of the states.)
- Congress can impeach and remove federal judges.
- The president appoints judges (who must be confirmed by the Senate).[8]

Why three branches? The idea of having three branches of government was birthed by the writings of Baron Charles Montesquieu, an authoritative French professor, author, and legal philosopher—who was the most often quoted source among the colonists next to the Bible.[9] His book *The Spirit of Laws* "greatly impacted the formation of the American government, as it was read and studied intently in America."[10] In it, Montesquieu acknowledges the deceit and wickedness of the human heart, as shown in Jeremiah 17:9, and advocates for a system that tries to check and moderate mankind's worse excesses by dividing power into three parts, inspired by Isaiah 33:22, which states, "For the LORD is our judge, the LORD is our lawgiver, the LORD is our king."

The real genius in the system of checks and balances established by the founders is that the executive branch—the branch most likely to become too powerful and "king-like"—is checked by the other two branches of government that did not want to be minimized. And in order for the system to be truly representative of the people, the representatives were intended to be integral members of their communities. The constituents of the House of Representatives and Senate were to be farmers, teachers, nurses, doctors, lawyers, businessmen, pharmacists, and—well, you get the picture. They were to represent every segment of society so that everyone's interests would be represented fairly. As long as you have broad representation from many parts of society, representative government works extremely well. And it works even better when the representatives serve for only a short period of time and return to their communities, leaving a spot for someone else from the community to become the next representative.

CHECKS OUT OF BALANCE

A couple of things can severely interfere with the efficacy of this system of checks and balances, however. One is when an elected representative becomes entrenched and wants to keep returning to the House of Representatives, becoming progressively less connected with the community that he or she represents. Although the founding fathers thought of many things, they failed to realize that the facet of human nature that makes people strive for power and influence might result in it becoming very difficult for them to give up their seat in the House of Representatives once they had it. The other detrimental thing is having one profession or group of individuals being overly represented. If there were too many doctors serving in and/ or represented in government, there would probably be an overabundance of health-related legislation; likewise, if there were too many farmers, there would likely be an abundance of agricultural legislation.

Perhaps as you've been reading you've wondered why a neurosurgeon is sharing his ideas about government when the training, education, and focus of a neurosurgeon's life is decidedly scientific and concerns biomedical dilemmas and solutions. You might be surprised to know that five physicians signed the Declaration of Independence, and many of them were involved with the creation of the United States Constitution. I believe it is a very good idea for physicians, scientists, engineers, and others trained to make decisions based on facts and empirical data to get involved in the political arena and help guide our country. Physicians were once much more involved in their communities and with governance in general. But in recent years we have tended to spend all of our time in our operating rooms, clinics, laboratories, and professional societies, leaving the governance to others. This is a mistake, because we should be concerned not only about the health of individual patients, but also about the health of our entire society. Since those in the health-care professions are among the most highly trained people in our society (a typical physician spends an average of over five years in postgraduate training), we should be willing to share the benefits of our education and critical thinking with the society that made it possible.

As it stands today we have too many lawyers in government—many of whom are very smart and decent people—but they are not immune from acting like lawyers. Consequently, we have far too much regulatory legislation. Also, what do many lawyers learn in law school? They learn to win by hook or by crook; it doesn't matter how you fight as long as you win. Imagine a roomful of Democratic and Republican lawyers, each with one overriding goal to win, and this certainly helps one understand the distasteful partisan politics that characterizes Congress today.

THAT UNINTENDED FOURTH BRANCH OF GOVERNMENT

Having three, well-balanced branches of government was an inspired and creative idea, but I do not believe that the founding fathers intended for a fourth branch of government to emerge—that of special interest groups. These groups would not have the great power they do today in the scenario originally envisioned by the founding fathers, in which dedicated citizens served in Congress for a few years and then returned to their original walks of life. But because many in Congress want to keep returning term after term, they need to constantly campaign and seek funding, much of which is obtained from special interest groups. Needless to say, money from these groups is not given without strings being attached. These tangled relationships have reached the point now where powerful corporate groups, unions, and other groups with large amounts of money to spend can exert great influence on the legislative process, which essentially pitches logical solutions to problems out the proverbial window, and favors solutions that benefit the special interest groups. This is an extremely serious problem, which threatens the very integrity of our system of government. I suspect that if the founding fathers were suddenly resurrected and saw the current situation, they would mandate a constitutional convention to find a solution to this problem posthaste!

One solution to the problem of special interest groups might be to lengthen the term one serves as a representative from two years to six, eight, or even ten years—with no possibility of reelection. You could couple that term length with a right of recall by the populace every other year if the representative were doing an exceptionally bad job. Congressmen could then govern based on the wishes of their constituents and pay little or no attention to special interest groups. Can you even imagine how much more efficiently and logically our government would work under such a circumstance?

A few years ago, my friend Dr. Henry Brem, who is the chairman of the neurosurgery department at Johns Hopkins, and I wrote an op-ed piece for the *Washington Post* focusing on tort reform. In that piece, we called for the media to focus attention on the United States senators who had been co-opted by the Trial Lawyers Association to the point that they would always filibuster any tort reform bill that came before the Senate. This is certainly an example of how the media could be very helpful by exposing not only the special interest groups and what they are doing, but also the leaders who are being influenced by them. Revealing this practice could discourage such close relationships between our elected officials and special interest groups.

The founding fathers certainly feared government becoming too big and too powerful. Observing this imbalance overseas, Thomas Jefferson wrote in a letter, "Experience declares that man is the only animal which devours his own kind; for I can apply no milder term to the governments of Europe, and to the general prey of the rich on the poor."[11]

When the American experiment appeared to be preparing to return to big government rule, ex-President George Washington wrote to Justice John Jay, astounded that the ideals that had been agonized over, rehashed, and reworked had fallen into a whirlpool of indifference:

> What astonishing changes a few years are capable of producing! I am told that even respectable characters speak of a monarchical form of government without horror. From thinking proceeds speaking, thence to acting is often but a single step. But how irrevocable and tremendous! What a triumph for the advocates of despotism to find that we are incapable of governing ourselves, and that systems founded on the basis of equal liberty are merely ideal and fallacious! Would to God that wise measures may be taken in time to avert the consequences we have but too much reason to apprehend.[12]

The founders realized that a gigantic government would require increasingly large amounts of resources from the people in the form of taxes, and that the people would consequently expect more from such a government since they were giving it so much of their money. Eventually government could become so big that its ravenous appetite for tax money coupled with a populace that expects so much from it creates a bloated, unsustainable system, no longer able to provide for itself. Many of the countries from which the founding fathers fled could be characterized in just this way, which is why they were so rightly concerned the United States would fall prey to the same problems.

Certainly the plight of such countries as Greece, Ireland, Italy, Portugal, and Spain have received a lot of attention recently[13] due to significant public outcries, demonstrations, and even riots because their governments have not been able to fulfill their promised social obligations to the people due to lack of funds, despite high tax rates. We could not ask for more timely examples of what happens when we abandon our founding principles of limited government and protecting individual rights.

OUR FREEDOMS: A SYSTEM BUILT TO CHANGE WITH THE TIMES

The founding fathers also knew they needed to design a system that would give the people flexibility to alter the government if it became too bloated. Freedom of speech and freedom of the press, as well as the right to peacefully assemble, were among the key provisions included to preserve our freedom. In many societies around the world, criticism of the government can result in imprisonment or death; in America, however, criticism occurs on a daily basis. In fact, our free press is one of the real virtues of American society. One of the greatest journalists of all time was Walter Cronkite, whose integrity was never questioned. Although his political leanings were decidedly left-wing, you would have had great difficulty detecting it because of his balanced treatment of the news.

I do not want to be overly critical of the news media today because I realize what a difficult task they have reporting news around the clock. When one has all day to talk about the news—and one *has* to talk about the news all day—it is hard not to offer personal commentary and, at times, embellish. Nevertheless, we the people should expect integrity from the news media and unbiased reporting of newsworthy events. When a news reporter or commentator can tell a flat-out lie and not be terminated or even required by the network to offer a public apology, we have a problem. I am still a big fan of our news media, however, and I certainly hope they can take corrective action on their own to preserve a noble profession.

The freedoms built into our Constitution actually give us power to dramatically change things about our society with which we disagree. For instance, in the 1950s and 1960s, segregation and racial discrimination were rampant in America. The populace became increasingly discontent with the glaring injustices they witnessed nightly on television. Many nonviolent protests were carried out, and the media did a magnificent job of highlighting the shortcomings of both federal and local governments in resolving the situation. As a result of these social movements and the courage of many individuals, a whole way of life that was a scourge upon our nation was changed. Protests and the media were also instrumental in ending the Vietnam War. As long as we have a courageous populace, and a courageous and unbiased media, we are likely to be able to correct significant societal problems as they arise, which is a part of the greatness of America. Unfortunately, political correctness threatens the integrity of the media, and we must all be vigilant in our attempt to continue the great experiment that is America.

IS THIS A GOVERNMENT BY THE PEOPLE, FOR THE PEOPLE?

The kind of government proposed by the framers of our Constitution was intended to serve the people. This meant providing protection, adequate infrastructure, the right to make a living, and the right to pursue happiness. The kind of government that the framers did not want was one that tried to control the lives of its constituents. They realized that the latter type of government would transform "we the people" from a "can do" society to a "what can you do for me" society.

It is really quite phenomenal how quickly America went from a lowly colony to the very pinnacle nation of the world. It happened because so many people were willing to work hard, not so much for themselves as for their children and their grandchildren. Many of them had emigrated from countries where hard work did not pay off, and they were excited to be in a place where they could actually realize the fruits of their own labor in a tangible way, improving the possibilities for their offspring.

Those who propelled our nation to the pinnacle status in a very short period of time also knew the importance of sacrifice. Now it sometimes seems our government leaders do not understand the concept of sacrifice. They have no problem with the *populace* sacrificing, but our federal government does not seem to know how to tighten its own belt, preferring to simply raise taxes to cover its own excesses. This would not be the case if our representatives in Congress were more in tune with their constituency. The current government is akin to a person who checks into a hotel and discovers that all of his bills are being taken care of by someone else, and so he feels free to live it up.

As long ago as 1791, Thomas Paine noted a similar situation in the governments of Europe. In his book *The Rights of Man* he observed the following:

> If from the more wretched parts of the old world, we look at those which are in an advanced stage of improvement, we still find the greedy hand of government thrusting itself into every corner and crevice of industry, and grasping the spoil of the multitude. Invention is continually exercised, to furnish new pretenses for revenues and taxation. It watches prosperity as its prey and permits none to escape without tribute.

Several of our founders had very strong opinions on this type of taxation. "To take from one," Thomas Jefferson wrote in a letter, "because it is thought his own industry and that of his fathers has acquired too much, in order to spare to others, who, or whose fathers, have not exercised equal industry and skill, is to violate arbitrarily the first principle of association, the guarantee to everyone the free exercise of his industry and the fruits acquired by it."[14]

Taxation is not the only way in which the government is out of step with the lives and wishes of the people. The overwhelming majority of Americans want the southern borders of our country secured and our immigration laws enforced, but several administrations recently have been unwilling to get tough on this issue because they do not want to alienate a large voting block of Latinos. This is yet another area where our government's leadership and the wishes of many of the people diverge and the people are being ignored.

When a government turns from following the will of its people to willing its people to follow—acting according to its own prerogatives—it ceases to be a representative government and instead has transformed into something else. One need only look back to one of our most foundational governing documents, the Declaration of Independence, to hear the founders' original intent for our nation: "Governments are instituted among men," wrote Thomas Jefferson, "deriving their just powers from the consent of the governed." Our unique governing process was laid out clearly and concisely in our Constitution, and for centuries it has successfully withstood the test of time. Because of its clear instructions for the transfer of power, administrations from our different parties have always transitioned smoothly, unlike most other countries.

But political and economic stability over a long period of time can breed complacency among its people, and Jefferson cautioned us that a government should be *by the people*. "Every government degenerates," he wrote in his book *Notes on the State of Virginia*, "when trusted to the rulers of the people alone. The people themselves, therefore, are its only safe depositories."[15] And in order to serve as those "safe depositories," we the people must keep ourselves informed and abreast of the actions of our governing leaders, speak out, and vote accordingly — lest our government lead us somewhere we have no desire to go.

—CHAPTER 3—

ARE WE A JUDEO-CHRISTIAN NATION OR NOT?

IN APRIL OF 1999, the world was shocked by the horrific murders at Columbine High School in Colorado. Some very close friends of ours were so deeply moved by the tragedy that they dedicated much of their lives and their substantial financial resources to making sure that good came out of the situation. This extraordinary couple gained the trust of the families who lost children in the shooting, as well as school officials and legal representatives, and they established a charity to promote character building in schools as a deterrent to the type of behavior that Columbine High had suffered.

The program plan was for students to select thirteen of the most desirable, positive character traits (in honor of the thirteen victims and in keeping with the thirteen colonies of the American Revolution), each of which was associated with an historical figure, such as "Honesty and Abe Lincoln." Students exemplifying these character traits would be rewarded each year. Due to my close relationship with these friends, and because I do a lot of public speaking for schools and educational organizations, I was asked to be the keynote speaker at Columbine for the rollout of the new program. I have spoken to all types of groups throughout this nation and many other parts of the world, but there was something particularly special about speaking at the site of such an infamous, evil event. Before actually going to the school, I met some who had survived the shooting as well as family members of victims. It seemed as if I knew them already since there had been so much publicity surrounding each victim. The brother of one of the young ladies who was killed—and who had narrowly escaped with his own life—was particularly articulate and a fabulous spokesperson for the group. He was a devout person of faith and a tremendous encouragement to me.

When I first stepped on campus I noticed that the school's hallways were incredibly sterile; there were no stickers, graffiti, or any other signs of the myriad ways that high school students usually decorate their environment. It had indeed been a war zone. I was told by some of the officials that all graffiti had been removed to ensure that no one was frightened or influenced to join a group that was not completely wholesome.

One of the officials indicated to me that they knew I was a man of faith, but that it would not be appropriate for me to talk about God or Jesus Christ. Although I did not show it outwardly, I was stunned, because I thought Columbine High School would be the last place on earth where I would hear such an admonition. Those officials were not bad people; quite the contrary. But they were extremely afraid of creating controversy or being blamed for what had occurred. I could tell that some of the administrators did not agree with this policy, but they wanted to maintain the harmony. I don't usually get nervous before a speech, but in this particular case I had received so many warnings about what not to say due to the sensitivity of the audience, that I was off my game.

The program was beautifully organized by our friends, the school officials, and students, and I was already quite inspired by the time I took the podium in the gymnasium before the entire school body, parents, officials, and the media. I spoke a bit about hardship and how it can be an advantage if one does not become a victim. I also commented about resilience and how success is frequently preceded by failure, but at the conclusion I had to talk about God and the very godly principles that resulted in the establishment of our great nation. At the end, I received a standing ovation from an incredibly enthusiastic crowd, and I knew that I had done the right thing by not hiding my faith or denying the principles that have led to well-functioning harmonious communities throughout our nation. Was I aware that I was violating the established protocols for the program? Of course I was. But I also knew that the whole purpose of the program was to promote character, and if I denied my faith I would be manifesting a total lack of character—for the sake of pleasing a few, I would have disappointed many.

One of the reasons public institutions would rather exclude God is to avoid offending others and creating controversy. They do not want Jews to be offended by the mention of the name Jesus Christ, nor do they want Muslims to be offended by the Torah, nor Christians to be offended by treks to Mecca.

The story of Abraham is well known to Jews, Christians, and Muslims; he is referred to as "the father" in all three religions. Yet even though there is a common ancestor, human nature and the desire for superiority has turned these differences into cause for war and mayhem. Historically, millions of people have been killed in the name of religion. The brutality associated with the Crusades, the Muslim conquests, the French Wars of Religion, the Reconquista, and, more recently, the Jihad illustrate how strongly people can feel about their religion. But can all this religious fervor be channeled in a positive rather than negative way?

As a Christian, I am not the least bit offended by the beliefs of Hindus, Buddhists, Muslims, Jehovah's Witnesses, Mormons, and so forth. In fact, I am delighted to know that they believe in something that is more likely to make them into a reasonable human being, as long as they don't allow the religion to be distorted by those seeking power and wealth.

Those in positions of leadership in our society must familiarize themselves with the religions of all their citizens, and they must begin to emphasize the commonalities that unite us as people of faith. Common objectives placed on the forefront of public policies will help people work together and bond us together as a nation in spite of our religious differences.

Another example that caused me to contemplate the question, are we a Judeo-Christian nation or not? was when I was asked to deliver the keynote address at the 1997 Presidential Prayer Breakfast in Washington, DC. This is of course a great honor, for the audience consists not only of the president, vice president, and their families, but Supreme Court justices, United States senators and congressmen, as well as ambassadors and dignitaries from every walk of life from all over the world. I became familiar with the Secret Service through many calls and emails, and everything had to be scripted down to the second. They had a hard time believing I was a spontaneous speaker and did not use notes. I was pretty excited about the speech until someone said to me that I should not mention the name of Jesus Christ. That seemed like a very strange request for a prayer breakfast.

In the receiving line in the pre-breakfast reception — the first time that I met President Clinton and his wife as well as the Gore family — my entire family had the opportunity to shake hands with the president and vice president, as well as meet many people you usually see only on the national evening news.

When it was my turn to speak, I briefly recounted my rise from inner-city poverty to the esteemed halls of Johns Hopkins. I talked about how education cultivates human potential and I spoke about integrity, particularly in public office. Coincidentally, I delivered this speech just before the Monica Lewinsky situation became public. The president must have been wondering, does he know what's going on? Obviously I did not know, but even if I had, I would have still made the same remarks. President Clinton, like all of us, had some weaknesses which got him into trouble. He is not the first public figure to have such troubles and certainly will not be the last. I suspect he would have been better served if he had simply confessed his wrongdoing and asked for forgiveness, but that of course is much easier said than done. Students of American history may recall that Alexander Hamilton had an affair while in public office, but when he quickly confessed publicly and was forgiven, the issue was pushed aside, much to the consternation of the mistress and her husband who were planning to blackmail Mr. Hamilton.

I finished the speech with my philosophy for success in life, which includes strong faith in God and my Savior Jesus Christ. The response was overwhelming, and the standing ovation lasted for several minutes, throwing the program off its strict time schedule. The president, in typical Clinton-esque style, took the microphone and asked, "Who is responsible for putting this guy on the program before me?" To which the crowd responded with raucous laughter. I subsequently got tons of mail complimenting me on what many felt was the best presidential prayer breakfast address they had ever heard. Out of the thousands of people at the breakfast, and millions of people who heard the address, I received only one negative response for using the name of Jesus. This tells me that the level of tolerance for religious differences is much greater than the politically correct crowd would have us believe.

FOUNDING FATHER, FULL OF FAITH

But what did the founders of our nation believe? Were they Christian believers in God or were they deists? A deist believes in God as a First Cause, a clockmaker who set up the universe to operate on its own. Deists do not believe in a God who intervenes in this world. By that standard, George Washington was by no means a Deist.

In *George Washington's Sacred Fire*, the former president is quoted in a letter written in May of 1789 to the General Assembly of Presbyterian Churches in the United States:

> While I reiterate the professions of my dependence upon Heaven as the source of all public and private blessings; I will observe that the general prevalence of piety, philanthropy, honesty, industry, and economy seems, in the ordinary course of human affairs, particularly necessary for advancing and conforming the happiness of our country.

> While all men within our territories are protected in worshipping the Deity according to the dictates of their consciences; it is rationally to be expected from them in return, that they will be emulous of evincing [striving to prove] the sanctity of their professions by the innocence of their lives and the beneficence of their actions; for no man who is profligate in his morals, or a bad member of the civil community can possibly be a true Christian, or a credit to his own religious society.[1]

The founding father of our country was definitely a believer in the God of the Bible, a man not only of tremendous intellect, but of conscience, caring, dedication, and faith. And his faith was founded on experience. One particularly interesting account occurred on July 9, 1755, during the French and Indian War. George Washington was with the British troops under General Edward Braddock on their way to Fort Duquesne when they were ambushed by the French. The Brits were being slaughtered since they were only accustomed to fighting in open fields. To deliver orders from General Braddock to the troops, Washington rode horseback back and forth across the battle. Every other officer on horseback, except Washington, was shot down. Even General Braddock was killed, at which point the troops fled in confusion. After the battle, on July 18, 1755, Washington wrote to his brother, John A. Washington: "But by the all-powerful dispensations of Providence, I have been protected beyond all human probability or expectation; for I had four bullets through my coat, and two horses shot under me, yet escaped unhurt, although death was leveling my companions on every side of me!"

Fifteen years later, Washington and Dr. Craik, a close friend of his from his youth, were traveling through those same woods near the Ohio River and Great Kanawha River. There they were met by an old Indian chief, who addressed Washington through an interpreter:

> I am a chief and ruler over my tribes. My influence extends to the waters of the great lakes and to the far blue mountains. I have traveled a long and weary path that I might see the young warrior of the great battle. It was on the day when the white man's blood mixed with the streams of our forests that I first beheld this chief [Washington]. I called to my young men and said, mark yon tall and daring warrior? He is not of the red-coat tribe — he hath an Indian's wisdom and his warriors fight as we do — himself alone exposed. Quick, let your aim be certain, and he dies. Our rifles were leveled, rifles which, but for you, knew not how to miss — 'twas all in vain, a power mightier far than we, shielded you. Seeing you were under the special guardianship of the Great Spirit, we

immediately ceased to fire at you. I am old and soon shall be gathered to the great council fire of my fathers in the land of shades, but ere I go, there is something bids me speak in the voice of prophecy: Listen! The Great Spirit protects that man [pointing at Washington], and guides his destinies—he will become the chief of nations, and a people yet unborn will hail him as the founder of a mighty empire. I am come to pay homage to the man who is the particular favorite of Heaven, and who can never die in battle.

A famous Indian warrior who was in that battle said, "Washington was never born to be killed by a bullet! I had seventeen fair fires at him with my rifle, and after all could not bring him to the ground!"[2]

Why was this history removed from school textbooks, which had included it up until 1934? As incredible a story as it may seem, it demonstrates the effect of having faith in God—for a person or even for a country. As George Washington himself said, "It is the duty of all Nations to acknowledge the providence of Almighty God, to obey his will, to be grateful for his benefits, and humbly to implore his protection and favors."[3]

ESCAPING PREJUDICES, PURSUING LIBERTIES

Many of the colonists had fled Europe to escape prejudices and to enjoy the liberty of worshiping according to their beliefs. But this was not necessarily the case for others, and George Washington was more open-minded than most in embracing those who had come to the New World for other reasons. One of his good friends, Haym Salomon, had immigrated from Poland in 1772 after having traveled throughout Europe. In a time when Jews were thought of as shylocks and money grubbers, George Washington recognized the solid character of Haym.

At that time, Congress had no powers of direct taxation and was struggling to raise money to support the war. Congress requested money from the states, but these requests were mostly refused. So perilous was the status of the army that they often lived day-to-day. The only choice left to our government was to borrow funds.

Haym Salomon, who became a very successful currency broker, used his financial savvy to finance the Revolution. Salomon volunteered his own fortune of 600,000 pounds sterling to begin the American Revolution—which today would be several million dollars, an immense fortune.[4]

When the British Parliament authorized covert financial tricks to undermine the colonists, such as counterfeiting colonial paper money and discrediting American envoys in Holland and France, they were hoping to cause

Washington's army to mutiny from lack of pay and necessities. But Salomon came through again with personal loans and brokered finance deals both in the New World and elsewhere around the world.

Salomon also proved his worth as a spy for George Washington as well as a finance man when he was captured by the British. When he noticed the British soldiers didn't speak German, and the German mercenaries who had been hired by the Brits didn't speak English, he informed the Brits of his knowledge of languages, without actually offering to translate. (He did not want to be seen as a Loyalist.) While interpreting, he then persuaded over five hundred Hessian soldiers from Germany to desert the British cause for the American side! Salomon also solicited every able-bodied Jewish man to fight in Washington's army. After the war, he organized the first American veterans' organization, "The Jewish War Veterans," which is still active today.

Michael Feldberg writes, "Within five years of his arrival in Philadelphia, Salomon advanced from penniless fugitive to respected businessman, philanthropist, and defender of his people. He risked his fortune, pledged his good name and credit on behalf of the Revolution, and stood up for religious liberty. Despite financial setbacks at the end of his life, Salomon's name is forever linked to the idealism and success of the American Revolution, and to the contributions Jews have made to the cause of American freedom."[5]

It is clear that significant Judeo-Christian influences were involved in the founding of our nation, although being a nation of all peoples, coming from different backgrounds and cultures, Christian, Jewish, and others, did not hinder us. Although it is difficult to verify, many believe that a star of David on the back of the one dollar bill is a tribute to Haym Salomon and the many Jewish Americans who fought for our initial freedom.

FAITH OF OUR FOUNDING FATHERS

Freedom of religion is one of the basic tenets of the founding of our nation, and while we are primarily a Judeo-Christian nation, we are a nation of faith that encompasses many religions and beliefs. We as a nation welcome all nonviolent people of every faith, and there was never any intention by our founders of excluding religion from our public or private lives. They did not want us to embrace a theocracy, but neither did they want us to eschew religious principles.

Our National Day of Prayer, for example, is a significant part of our heritage. In 1775, during a meeting of the Continental Congress, all of the colonies were asked to pray for wisdom as the policies to govern the nation were being formed. During the Civil War, President Lincoln proclaimed a day of "humiliation, fasting and prayer," and in 1952, President Truman signed a joint resolution from the Congress officially creating a National Day of Prayer.

Undoubtedly, there are some in our country who are very uncomfortable with the highest levels of our government recognizing and encouraging prayer, but as Mrs. Shirley Dobson, who was chairman of the National Day of Prayer, put it, "We have lost many of our freedoms in America because we have been asleep. I feel if we do not become involved and support the annual National Day of Prayer, we could end up forfeiting this freedom too."[6] However, in April 2010, US district judge Barbara Crabb in Wisconsin ruled that the government-sanctioned National Day of Prayer, established by Congress and supported with a proclamation from the president, is unconstitutional.

I believe the problem arises from misinterpretation of what our founders intended with respect to government and religion. Having lived in Europe's Old World they were very familiar with the deleterious effects of state-sponsored religion. They never wanted to see the government endorse a specific religion, but neither did they want to see faith and religion suppressed. There is nothing at all in our founding documents forbidding or denigrating religious expression in public life. The judge in this case was responding to a lawsuit filed by a group of atheists and agnostics called the Freedom from Religion Foundation. They complained that the government did not have the right to tell them to pray, but perhaps they didn't notice that prayer was not a requirement, but rather a suggestion. A government requirement would be something like paying your income taxes. If you owe taxes and refuse to pay them, you will quickly learn the difference between a suggestion and a requirement.

Speaking on the separation of church and state, Joel Oster, senior counsel for the Alliance Defense Fund, added, "The National Day of Prayer provides an opportunity for all Americans to pray voluntarily according to their own faith—it does not violate the establishment clause of the First Amendment."[7] Not only have polls shown that most Americans feel positive about a national day of prayer, but interestingly a Rasmussen report from February 2010 showed that 65 percent of Americans prefer having prayer in schools! Unfortunately, the very vocal minority trying to suppress religious expression in America has been successful in getting this issue to the top of the political correctness list. Even though most Americans believe in God and many have a strong personal faith, political correctness decries public declarations of that faith. Yet even both houses of Congress begin each session with public prayer. Because I do a lot of public speaking, people regularly thank me for being bold about my belief in God. If most people believe in God and yet we are afraid to speak of that belief in public, what does that say about the freedoms that our ancestors fought and died for?

At the Constitutional Convention of 1787, Benjamin Franklin, who was eighty-one years old, gave the following address on June 28 when hostilities and bitterness threatened to totally disrupt the convention:

> Mr. President: the small progress we have made after four or five weeks close attendance and continual reasoning with each other — our different sentiments on almost every question, several of the last producing as many noes as ayes, is methinks a melancholy proof of the imperfection of the human understanding.
>
> We indeed seem to feel our own want of political wisdom, since we have been running about in search of it. We have gone back to ancient history for models of government, and examined the different forms of those republics which, having been formed with the seeds of their own dissolution, no longer exist. And we have viewed modern states all round Europe, but find none of their constitutions suitable to our circumstances.
>
> In this situation of our assembly, groping as it were in the dark to find political truth, and scarce able to distinguish it when presented to us, how has it happened, sir, that we have not hitherto once thought of humbly applying to the Father of lights to illuminate our understanding? In the beginning of the contest with Great Britain, when we were sensible of danger, we had daily prayer in this room for divine protection. Our prayers, sir, were heard, and they were graciously answered. All of us who were engaged in the struggle must have observed frequent instances of a superintending Providence in our favor.
>
> To that kind Providence we owe this happy opportunity of consulting in peace on the means of establishing our future national felicity. And have we now forgotten that powerful Friend? Or do we imagine we no longer need His assistance? I have lived, sir, a long time, and the longer I live, the more convincing proofs I see of this truth — that God governs in the affairs of men. And if a sparrow cannot fall to the ground without His notice, is it probable that an empire can rise without His aid?
>
> We had been assured, sir, in the sacred writings, that "except the Lord build the house they labor in vain that build it." I firmly believe this; and I also believe that without His concurring aid we shall succeed in this political building no better than the builders of Babel: we shall be divided by our partial local interests, our projects will be confounded,

and we ourselves have become a reproach and byword down to future ages. And what is worse, mankind may hereafter from this unfortunate instance, despair of establishing governments by human wisdom and leave it to chance, war, and conquest.

I therefore beg leave to move—that henceforth prayers imploring the assistance of Heaven, and its blessing on our deliberations, be held in this assembly every morning before we proceed to business, and that one or more of the clergy of this city be requested to officiate in that service.[8]

The speech apparently had such a profound effect on all present that the assembly voted to begin every session with prayer, a tradition that has continued until this day. I love to drag this passage out when so-called intellectuals claim that Benjamin Franklin was an atheist. Many people like to rewrite history or delete portions to bolster their arguments before gullible audiences. But I am so grateful for people such as former congressional candidate William Federer, who has done extraordinary research to uncover documents revealing the true sentiments and beliefs of our founders. Only through the careful study of historical documents can we prevent the distortion of where we came from and who we are as a nation.

Freedom to worship or not worship as one pleases would not be an issue were it not for the extreme intolerance of antireligion groups. In many cases, these are the very same people who brand anyone who disagrees with their agenda as bigoted and intolerant. Their extreme hypocrisy is almost comical, were it not so sad.

I have also frequently heard people question the faith of Thomas Jefferson. However, in his 1781 notes on the state of Virginia, he wrote, "God who gave us life gave us liberty. And can the liberties of a nation be thought secure when we have removed their only firm basis, a conviction in the minds of the people that these liberties are of the gift of God? That they are not to be violated but with His wrath? Indeed, I tremble for my country when I reflect that God is just; that His justice cannot sleep forever."

This passage and many others like it leave no doubt about Jefferson's beliefs. There are many more convincing statements by other founding leaders such as George Washington, John Adams, Alexander Hamilton, Daniel Webster, Thomas Paine, John Locke, James Madison, and others that make it clear there was never any intention of removing God from the public sphere of our nation.[9]

Remember all the controversy in 2003 surrounding the order given by a United States district judge to remove the Ten Commandments monument from the rotunda of the Alabama State judicial building? A similar thing then happened in the courthouse in Jackson County, Kentucky, where the Ten Commandments had to be removed in response to a lawsuit. Statues, nativity scenes, and other religious objects have also been removed by zealous opponents of anything that has to do with God. Somehow the people initiating these lawsuits believe that making these objects visible to the public violates the establishment clause of the First Amendment to the Constitution, which says the legislature should make no law respecting an establishment of religion. They conveniently forget about that part of the amendment that follows saying that the government should not prohibit the free exercise of religion. The infamous lawsuit instigated by Michael Newdow in Sacramento sought to remove the phrase "under God" from the Pledge of Allegiance, but if these kinds of activities don't constitute the prohibition of free exercise of religion, then what does? Until the antireligion zealots learn the meaning of the word *tolerance*, we will continue to experience unnecessary strife.

What message are we sending the next generation when a student is not allowed to express himself freely? In the Morgan v. Plano Independent School District case, also known as the "candy cane" case, several students were denied their free speech rights and discriminated against because their speech was religious in nature. A young boy was singled out and banned from handing out candy cane pens with a religious message at his class "winter" party. This case also includes a little girl who was threatened for handing out tickets after school to a religious play, and an entire class of kids was forbidden from writing "Merry Christmas" on holiday cards to American troops serving overseas. The government officials who appealed the ruling are now arguing that elementary students are too young to have First Amendment rights.[10]

If anyone is still skeptical about our roots as a nation of faith, consider the fourth stanza of our national anthem:

Oh! Thus be it ever, when freemen shall stand
Between their loved homes and the war's desolation,
Blest with vict'ry and peace, may the heav'n-rescued land
praise the pow'r that hath made and preserved us a nation.
Then conquer we must, for our cause is just,
And this be our motto — "In God is our trust."
And the star-spangled banner in triumph doth wave
O'er the land of the free and the home of the brave.

Is it any wonder that God has blessed America to such a great extent? We acknowledge him in our founding document, the Declaration of

Independence, in our Pledge of Allegiance, in our courtrooms, in our national anthem, and on our money, to name a few things. In return, he has blessed us above all nations just as he said he would. Before we throw away those blessings, remember what George Washington said: "The man must be bad indeed who can look upon the events of the American Revolution without feeling the warmest gratitude toward the great Author of the Universe whose divine interposition was so frequently manifested in our behalf. And it is my earnest prayer that we may so conduct ourselves as to merit a continuance of those blessings with which we have hitherto been favored."[11]

Could it be that the father of our nation was not only talking to the people who were his contemporaries, but was also providing a word of encouragement and warning for future generations?

—CHAPTER 4—

A DIFFERENT SCHOOL OF THOUGHT

ON MY FIRST DAY in Mrs. McQueen's bright, cheery kindergarten class at Detroit's Fisher Elementary School, all students were required to bring a rug on which to sit while we happily learned new songs, games, and facts all day long. Since my mother was (and still is) so thrifty, she was able to supply one for me in spite of the fact that we didn't have much money. At the time, I didn't think about the fact that it probably came from either Goodwill or the Salvation Army; I was simply excited about the new experience and the opportunity to play with so many other children.

Kindergarten, first, second, and the first half of third grade were not particularly rigorous. School was mostly fun and games, I was an average student, and life was peaceful. After my parents got divorced and we were forced to move to Boston, we lived in a tenement not far from Franklin Park and the Zoo. My brother, Curtis, and I walked through the park every morning on our way to a parochial school, which had only two classrooms. There were four grades in each classroom, and all eight grades were taught by only two teachers. Consequently, the vast majority of our time was spent singing songs and playing games.

By the time my mother, Curtis, and I moved back to Detroit, I had essentially lost a year of school while in Boston, my academic performance lagging far behind that of my new classmates. To make matters worse, I was the only black kid in the class. In those days in Detroit, academic expectations for a black boy were not very high, particularly in a predominantly white school. After every quiz, each student had to report his or her score out loud for the teacher to record, and classmates always snickered after I announced my abysmally low scores. Although they teased me a great deal about this, none of them ever had to worry about getting the lowest score on a test as long as I was in the classroom. You might say I served as the class safety net.

Needless to say, my self-esteem began to follow my academic expectations of myself in a downward spiral. I would even laugh along with others at some of the jokes about me. To cope with the ridicule, I smiled a lot and tried to adopt a nonchalant attitude about being the class dummy. I secretly admired those who always knew the answers and were the last ones out in the spelling bees. I never imagined that I could be smart, let alone win a spelling bee. The low expectations everyone had for me—including my own expectations of myself—would certainly have predicted a dismal future for me.

Fortunately my mother, with her third-grade education, was terrified that because of our poor academic performance both my brother and I would end up with low-paying menial jobs as she had. She didn't know what to do to help change our path, so she asked God to give her wisdom on how to inspire her sons to work hard and make something of themselves. That's when she came up with the idea of turning off the television and making us read two books apiece from the Detroit public libraries each week. She also made us submit to her written book reports, which of course she could not read, but we didn't know that. Her friends told her that her sons would grow up to hate her, but that did not matter to her, as long as we were successful.

I didn't hate Mother, but in the beginning I sure hated reading those books. After a while, however, I actually began to look forward to them, because they afforded me a fantastic escape from our everyday poverty and sense of hopelessness. There in the city, books about nature captivated me. First I read *Chip, The Dam Builder*, then other animal stories over the years up to Jack London's *Call of the Wild* as my reading ability increased. I began to imagine myself as a great explorer or scientist or doctor. I learned things no one else around me knew. Every single day my knowledge of our world expanded, which excited me to no end. And since I was constantly reading, I became a much better speller and started becoming competitive in the spelling bees.

Once I started believing I was smart, I really didn't care that much about what anybody else thought about me, and I became consumed with a desire to increase my learning far beyond that of my classmates. The more I read biographies about those who had made significant accomplishments in life, the more I wanted to emulate them. By the time I reached the seventh grade, I reveled in the fact that the same classmates who used to taunt me were now coming to me, asking how to solve problems or spell words. Once the joy of learning filled my heart, there was no stopping me.

Many of the teachers at Southwestern High School in Detroit were excellent, but they rarely had the opportunity to demonstrate how good they were because so much of classroom time was wasted handling disciplinary problems. I remember seeing teachers in tears because of the treatment they received from students trying to show off for others. Things almost turned violent when a substitute was once unfortunate enough to be cast into the "den of lions." The young teacher assigned to one of my history classes had the glasses, tweed jacket, brown shoes, and short pants to suggest that he was a nerd, and the students could not wait to begin tormenting him with odd noises, paper wads, and wisecracks. He became so frustrated that he left the room, and the assistant principal had to come restore order. The same scenario was repeated over and over again in my biology class with Mr. McCotter, a very nice man with a big heart, who wanted nothing more than to impart a solid education to the students who mercilessly tormented him. In spite of the resistance he faced, he never left the class and continued trying to teach against the odds. Given the challenges facing teachers such as these, it isn't hard to understand why Detroit has such low high school graduation rates.[1]

In spite of her exhaustion from working to make ends meet, Mother was dedicated to making sure Curtis and I would buck the trend, and if we were still up when she arrived home from work, she never neglected to ask what we had learned in school that day. Because of all the reading she had encouraged me to do, I was very motivated to learn and took it upon myself to achieve a first-class education in a second-class environment. I would go back after school to talk to any teacher whose lesson had been derailed by interruptions and ask, "What were you planning to teach today?" They would of course be delighted to share with me what they had prepared, and very much appreciated someone benefiting from their hard work.

Dedicated to placing myself in positions in which my education would flourish, I subsequently became the biology laboratory assistant and was responsible for setting up the laboratory experiments. This meant that, regardless of what lessons did or did not take place in class on any given day, I learned them nevertheless. Not long after that, I began helping set up some of the chemistry and physics laboratories as well.

My own initiative to learn was also encouraged by many of my teachers, who had a profound effect on my education. Mrs. Miller, one of my English teachers, took a strong interest in my academic performance and had tremendous influence in my life, frequently acting as a barrier between me and my recurrent desire to be part of the crowd. And many of my other teachers encouraged me to take part in the regional forensics contests, citywide competitions in which students from various schools had an opportunity to recite poetry or dramatic prose before an audience who rated them in terms of style and effectiveness. There I acquired a great deal of confidence in my ability to speak in public.

I also received help and guidance to participate in many of the citywide and statewide science fairs. These competitions exposed me to students from more affluent areas who were considerably more advanced than I was, inspiring me to work even harder.

One need look no further for public servants than the many public school teachers around our country. The vast majority of them not only pour themselves tirelessly into their work for the sake of their students, they also forgo all kinds of recognition and financial compensation to do so. When I won a scholarship to Interlochen, one of the most prestigious music camps in the country, instead of being elated that Southwestern High School had finally produced this level of musical talent, my band teacher, Mr. Doakes (who went on to become Dr. Doakes), advised me not to accept the scholarship "because it would interfere with my preparation to become a great doctor one day." He was willing to forgo a huge feather in his own cap for the sake of my career. Teachers like him were not uncommon as I was growing up, and it is one of the reasons why I have so much respect and admiration for teachers today.

Intending to become a citizen of the world, I extended my own education far beyond the school's curriculum. I began frequenting art museums, historical societies, and many of the collections and galleries found on campuses of local colleges and universities. I became quite an expert in identifying classical music, and both art and music remain an important part of my life today.

Through education, I was completely changed to become a productive citizen of the world. And what is true in the life of one is true in the life of whole communities and entire nations: education has the power to transform. I firmly believe that the solid public education system established in the American colonies centuries ago was largely responsible for our nation's rapid rise on the world stage in the areas of economics, innovation, and industry. And what was possible then is still possible today.

Valuing Education, Then and Now

Whenever an election is at hand, there is a lot of talk about the importance of education—but with a national high school dropout rate of 30 percent, we do not seem to be making much progress. A lot of talk may be just what it is. Our society is quite willing to spend hundreds of millions of dollars on a new stadium for the city's football or baseball team, while leaving many of the same city's public schools in a dilapidated condition with tattered books—and in some cases no books at all. Our young people see through this hypocrisy and tend to emulate what they *see* more than what they are *told*.

It was not always like this, however. Our nation's founders placed so much emphasis on education that towns in Massachusetts could actually be fined for not providing adequate public education. As early as 1642, a law was passed by the Massachusetts Bay Colony making education a requirement for children.[2] Compulsory education was much slower to reach the southern states,[3] and education of slaves was forbidden.[4] The very fact that powerful men in the South went to great lengths to prevent slaves from gaining an education makes it clear that they fully understood how empowering education can be. This fact alone should encourage anyone who is poor, weak, and/or powerless to direct all their energy toward obtaining an education.

The fact of the matter is, our founding fathers were highly educated individuals, many of whom had extensive personal libraries—and most of them had a vast knowledge of world history. They were not people of average intelligence. And as they were crafting the policies of our new nation, they designed a system that would work well only with an educated populace. This is why they emphasized the importance of a solid education.

In fact, when Frenchman Alexis de Tocqueville arrived in America in 1831 to decipher the secrets of our enormous economic success, he was so taken with our school system that he wrote extensively about what he saw as a unique and powerful tool to fuel a productive new nation. Unlike schools in Europe, American schools taught the children values, he noticed, and there was extensive use of the holy Bible in public schools. He wrote in *Democracy in America*:

> Upon my arrival in the United States the religious aspect of the country was the first thing that struck my attention; and the longer I stayed there, the more I perceived the great political consequences resulting from this new state of things. In France I had almost always seen the spirit of religion and the spirit of freedom marching in opposite

directions. But in America I found they were intimately united and that they reigned in common over the same country.[5]

He was particularly impressed by the fact that anyone finishing the second grade could read and write quite well. Even when he explored the frontiers, he was astonished to find common men engaging in intelligent conversation, reading the newspaper, and understanding the various branches of government. He also reflected:

> I sought for the key to the greatness and genius of America in her harbors ... in her fertile fields and boundless forests, in her rich mines and vast world commerce; in her public school system and institutions of learning. I sought for it in her democratic Congress and in her matchless Constitution. Not until I went into the churches of America and heard her pulpits flame with righteousness did I understand the secret of her genius and power. America is great because America is good, and if America ever ceases to be good, America will cease to be great.[6]

To gain a real appreciation of what children were expected to know in early America, one has only to look up an exit exam from middle school grades during the nineteenth century. I suspect that many, if not most, college graduates today would fail that test. Some sample questions:

- Describe three of the most prominent battles of the Rebellion.
- Name events connected with the following dates: 1607, 1620, 1800, 1849, and 1865.
- Show the territorial growth of the US.
- Name and locate the principal trade centers of the US.
- Name all the republics of Europe and give the capital of each.
- Describe why the Atlantic Coast is colder than the Pacific at the same latitude.

Over the ensuing decades, the American system of public education was admired throughout the world because of the quality of its products — its very citizens, well educated and ready to engage with the growth of their new nation.

THE DECLINE OF US EDUCATION

In the mid–twentieth century, however, a series of things began to happen that negatively impacted the quality of public education in the US. Public prayer was banned in school, and the educational agenda began to expand significantly beyond basic reading, writing, and arithmetic. By the early 1990s, a multinational study to determine the ability of eighth-grade equivalents in twenty-two different countries to solve complex math and science problems found that students in the United States ranked number twenty-one out of twenty-two. That the pinnacle nation in the world would have such a poor academic showing is not only embarrassing but extremely frightening.

When we instill morals and values into the educational process for young people, however, we help them realize they have an obligation to become well educated and informed citizens, and to contribute to the system as opposed to draining it of its resources. Public prayer and discussion of common principles that strengthen society's moral fabric are essential to establishing an atmosphere of courtesy and decency. The renowned Noah Webster said, "Society requires that the education of youth should be watched with the most scrupulous attention. Education, in a great measure, forms the moral characters of men, and morals are the basis of government."[7]

Today in the age of information and technology, "knowledge is power" more than ever before in the history of the world. Certainly during the Agricultural Age, the United States was able to produce so much corn, wheat, and barley that we became known as the breadbasket of the world. But we are no longer in the Agricultural Age. The Industrial Age followed, during which the United States blossomed into a giant that could produce more cars, airplanes, washing machines, and weapons than anyone thought possible — changing the course of the world for the better. But we are no longer in the Industrial Age. We now find ourselves in the Information Age, where academic accomplishment is more important than ever.

Today we produce only 60,000 to 70,000 engineers per year, 40 percent of whom are foreigners, while China produces over 400,000 engineers per year. With this kind of technological discrepancy, we will be left far behind in the not too distant future unless we begin to address our educational shortcomings with more than political rhetoric. China is not a democracy, and its emergence as a rising superpower will radically change the geopolitical landscape of the world.

Even if young people are not concerned about their role in world affairs, they should clearly be concerned about their own future economic well-being. Everyone should realize that today the average person lives to be about eighty years of age, the first twenty to twenty-five of which are used to either prepare oneself educationally — or not. For those who prepare well, about sixty years shall follow to reap the benefits; but for those who fail to prepare, there are sixty years to suffer the consequences. When you look at it that way, sacrificing a bit of fun and idleness early on can pay big dividends in the long run. Furthermore, as of 1999, a US Census Bureau report entitled "The Big Payoff: Educational Attainment and Synthetic Estimates of Work-Life Earnings" revealed that over an adult's working life (ages twenty-five through sixty-four), a high school graduate can expect to earn an average of $1.2 million. A college graduate will earn $2.1 million, while someone with a master's degree will earn $2.5 million. A person with a doctoral degree will earn $3.4 million, and those with professional degrees—such as medical, dental, or veterinary degrees—will earn $4.4 million on average. Obviously there has been some relative advance on those numbers since 1999, further underscoring the point.

EVERY OUNCE OF AMERICA'S TALENT MATTERS

Some readers may be thinking, *I have worked hard and achieved a lot in my personal life, so why should I worry myself about the well-being of people who are too lazy to take advantage of opportunities to succeed?* However, for every one of those young people we can keep from choosing a self-destructive path, that's one less person we have to be afraid of or protect our families from, one less person we will have to pay for in the penal system or the welfare system, and one more productive, taxpaying member of society who may discover a new energy source or the cure for cancer. Every person is endowed with God-given abilities, and we must cultivate every ounce of talent we have in order to maintain our pinnacle position in the world.

Our nation's founding fathers certainly believed in the task of educating the populace as foundational to a nation's health. In a letter to George Chapman on December 15, 1784, George Washington wrote, "The best means of forming a manly, virtuous, and happy people will be found in the right education of youth. Without this foundation, every other means, in my opinion, must fail." James Madison added, "A popular government, without popular information, or the means of acquiring it, is but a prologue to a farce or a tragedy; or, perhaps both. Knowledge will forever govern ignorance: and a people who mean to be their own governors, must arm themselves with the power which knowledge gives."[8]

These statements by some of our founding fathers emphasize how essential a solid general education is to all the constituents of American society. By remaining ignorant, we shirk our democratic duty and open ourselves to slick politicians who would usurp our rights. Some of the segments of our society who are most easily led astray are those with the poorest general education, which makes one wonder if those seeking political advantage are happy to maintain the status quo in order that the uneducated might be more easily manipulated.

The founders also believed that education is crucial to offering checks and balances to governing leaders' power. Otherwise, the insidious loss of freedom, quite relevant to us today, will follow. For "enlightened statesmen will not always be at the helm,"[9] James Madison noted in *The Federalist Papers*. He also pointed out in a speech to the Virginia ratifying convention on June 16, 1788, that "there are more instances of the abridgment of the freedom of the people by gradual and silent encroachments of those in power than by violent and sudden usurpations."

We can certainly see a gradual erosion of hard-won rights everywhere around us today. For instance, a recent regulation imposed by the Department of Veterans Affairs banned the words *God* and *Jesus* during funeral services at the Houston National Cemetery. This obvious violation of the Constitution is being challenged legally by the Veterans of Foreign Wars, the American Legion, and the National Memorial Ladies, who fortunately are educated enough to know their rights and are brave enough to fight for them.

I'm sure our nation's founders hoped and prayed that we would not stray from the freedom they fought and died to provide. Reading about their vision for a unique nation inhabited by people with unprecedented freedom is truly inspiring, and we must be careful not to allow those who like to rewrite history to silence the voices of those God-fearing visionaries who founded America. We have a very rich history of placing tremendous value on education, and there is no reason that we cannot once again become the world's most educated nation.

We have a tremendous amount of technology available to us that can help us quickly close the achievement gap that exists between our children and those in many other advanced nations. One such technology currently being developed is a computer program that analyzes the way a student solves math problems to figure out where there are gaps in that student's knowledge. The computer then tutors the student in his or her area of deficiency until the student is able to solve problems correctly. This is, of course, the same thing that a good teacher can do, but computers provide the ability to tutor a whole classroom simultaneously as opposed to one student at a time, allowing the teacher freedom to focus energy on students needing personal attention. We also should put a great deal of emphasis on the concept of virtual classrooms. Although the technology is only in its infancy, it will provide the ability to put the very best teachers in the world in front of millions of our children on the same day. It will allow children to virtually explore the pyramids of Egypt, or the Amazon Basin, or even the surface of the moon. This kind of education should also be available to parents and other adults who want to know what their children are learning and desire to increase their own value, because knowledge is power. Not only *can* we do this, but we *must* do this in order to remain a potent worldwide leader in this age of information.

CHAPTER 5

CAPITALISM:
ITS PROS AND CONS

EVERYONE HATES SOMETHING. Some hate spiders; others hate lizards or snakes, but I hated poverty. Growing up near the Delray and River Rouge neighborhoods of inner-city Detroit, and the Roxbury section of Boston gave me an up-close and personal view of poverty. I hated being poor, and I was eager to find a way out.

Living in run-down housing joined at common walls meant we could hear our neighbors on both sides of us, so sleep came only when voices settled down, if they did at all. On some nights, especially weekends, parties extended far into the morning hours. Break-ins and burglaries were common in the neighborhood, so we fortified our home with locks, bars, alarms, and a dog, which we particularly needed when my father left Mom and us two boys when I was eight. Living in that neighborhood, we felt unprotected, vulnerable at night, and alone.

The neighborhood housing projects I walked through when I began attending school in Boston were in even worse shape than ours. Some of the houses were abandoned, some were burned, and others were literally falling down altogether. But worse than the structural decay was the angry, aggressive attitude spawned by the conditions of poverty around us. No one seemed to care about the next guy, except to shake him down for money or maybe drugs. My brother, Curtis, and I were frequently bullied, and with Dad gone, Mom had to work multiple jobs just to provide. She never failed to put food on the table, however, and believed fervently that God would keep us going. I marveled at her faith, but I also wished she didn't have to work so hard. I wished better for her and for all of us.

I hated wearing secondhand clothing and loathed going to the store to buy groceries with food stamps. If I was at the counter and someone I knew was nearby, I would get out of line as if I had forgotten something, hoping that by the time I got back to the counter no one I knew would see me paying with food stamps. In hindsight, I see this was false pride and ignorance, since many of my peers probably used the stamps too, but hatred of poverty put enough fire in me to make me work hard to escape it.

Poverty bred the attitude in me that I was a nobody, that I was going nowhere, and that I probably would never get out. So I quit school mentally before I even started. I still walked the distance from our house to the school building; Mom made sure of that. But I was lazy. I was at the bottom of my class. And most of the kids in school loved to call me by the pet name "Dummy."

That's when I really began to see how my feelings about poverty could affect my attitude. I developed a violent, uncontrollable temper and my grades plummeted. When Mom found out I was failing the fifth grade and that my brother, Curtis, wasn't doing any better, she immediately instituted a program of little or no TV. We were told to focus on our homework, read books, and do book reports for her every week. Mom wanted out of the poverty too, and she knew that if we applied ourselves, we could climb out, something she had been unable to do herself. She couldn't read the reports we wrote, but we never knew that, and the hard work paid off.

From all I observed around me growing up and all I read, I quickly realized that, in spite of the circumstances affecting you, the person who had the most to do with what happened to you in life was you. If I wanted to escape poverty, I was going to have to work extremely hard, but this was within my grasp to accomplish. And in a place such as America, no one could stop me except myself.

I nearly had stopped myself through my belief that I would never amount to anything. But instead of choosing to fuel my anger further, I turned to books as a way out. As I read about explorers, entrepreneurs, industrial leaders, and inventors, I saw a common thread in their lives of the desire and ability to work hard in order to accomplish something. I was particularly inspired by the story of Booker T. Washington, who was born a slave. It was illegal for him to read, yet he taught himself and read everything in sight. Because of that commitment to continually better his life, he eventually became an advisor to two presidents.

The story of Joseph in the Bible's Old Testament impressed me even more. Sold into slavery by his own brothers, he didn't hold a pity party for himself. Instead he decided that if he was going to be a slave, he would be the best slave around. Because of his industriousness and dependability, he went on to become the head of the household of Potiphar, who was captain of the Egyptian guard. Even though Joseph was unjustly imprisoned for a second time because of Potiphar's wife's false accusation—something that might have derailed even the most determined person, pushing him toward a victim mentality—Joseph did not feel sorry for himself. Instead he put to work those same characteristics in the prison that had enabled him to achieve a high position in Potiphar's household. He soon had a very responsible position, and showing a skill in interpreting others' dreams, gained the attention of the pharaoh. Ultimately he became the governor of all of Egypt.

Reading about individuals such as these profoundly affected my work ethic and made me realize that I could easily change my destiny with determined personal effort. I did not have to depend on what someone else did or what someone else gave me in order to be successful. The only thing I really needed was the opportunity to work hard and display my talents. As long as there was no one there trying to stop me or confiscate the benefits of my labor, I was willing to enthusiastically pursue my goals.

CAPITALISM: PROS AND CONS

The United States of America is the most prolific example of capitalism in the history of the world. But what exactly is capitalism? You can find many different definitions, but they all point to the fact that capitalism is an economic system in which individuals or corporate groups have the right to make private decisions and to acquire private property and capital goods based on their own work and competition in a free market. In recent years, there has been a lot of debate about whether a capitalist or socialist government would best suit the people of our nation. People are social creatures who prefer to work together, play together, eat together, and share together—but do the basic tenets of capitalism preclude these natural tendencies?

Many opponents of capitalism say that the capitalist system fosters greed and selfishness and does not look out for the welfare of one's fellow man. If that were true, however, then the United States would have quickly dissolved into a hopelessly failed state instead of becoming the wealthiest and most powerful nation that the world has ever known.

You may be surprised to learn that it was the rapid rise of the United States as an economic power in the world that gave birth to the ideals of socialism. Many individuals in Europe and in other parts of the world were quite alarmed by the fact that relatively few people in America were making enormous sums of money while the great masses lived in poverty. They felt that it was quite unfair to have families such as the Vanderbilts, the Rockefellers, the Carnegies, the Mellons, the Kelloggs, and the Fords living lavishly, while the people around them suffered. Critics did acknowledge that these capitalists developed technologies that led to the creation of enormous wealth, but they felt that the level of wealth should be more fairly controlled and distributed by an overarching governmental agency. What those critics perhaps failed to understand is how much money each of the aforementioned families plowed back into the development of infrastructure and industries for our nation, creating an enormous number of jobs and opportunities for others to develop wealth.

Not only did America very quickly become a great economic and industrial power, but it also gave birth to the largest and most productive middle class the world had ever seen. In order for many of the businesses to succeed, it was necessary to produce in very large quantities, which of course required a great number of workers who had to be paid. Some companies were very fair to their workers and tended to do quite well; others had to be forced to be fair by unions, while still others were blatantly unfair and, in the long run, frequently suffered the consequences of such actions. Another phenomenon occurred in America which was unfamiliar to the Europeans—namely the advent of numerous charitable foundations created to aid the poor and to provide opportunities for the general populace. Obviously there was something different about the wealthy in America that distinguished them from the wealthy people in other parts of the world.

No matter how much of a fan of socialism or communism one is, it is difficult to deny the fact that entrepreneurship and inventive genius in America had a very profound effect on civilizations and living conditions throughout the world in a very short period of time. America had created an environment that provided incentive for people to come up with more and better ways of doing things. Jan Matzeliger, for example, was an African American who invented the shoe-lasting machine, revolutionizing the shoe industry and making shoes affordable by the masses with his 1883 patent.[1]

The establishment and protection of individual rights, woven into the founding values of our nation, extended into our business practices. The knowledge that you could acquire things for yourself and for your family by your own hard work and that those things would not be confiscated by another party was a powerful stimulus to economic activity, which quickly propelled America to the pinnacle of economic power in the world.

People throughout the world came to envy the American standard of living, and this country became the dream destination for poor immigrants everywhere.

GREED IS A FUNCTION OF THE HUMAN HEART

If the story ended there, the capitalist economic model would be declared the winner and we would all live happily ever after. Unfortunately, one of the tendencies of human nature, namely greed, often results in excessive profit taking at the expense of others.

Many years ago, a friend of mine received an academic scholarship to obtain his engineering degree at the City College of New York; however, the scholarship did not include room and board. So he was forced to live on the streets for a while, though he still maintained a healthy grade point average. For several months, he would even sneak into the professor's lounge in the evening and hide behind one of the couches until the room was locked at night. There he would sleep behind the couch and then sneak out in the morning once the lounge was unlocked. Having access to water and a bathroom helped, but he was even more delighted when snacks were left in the lounge.

After he finished his engineering degree, he went to work for the Federal Aviation Administration (FAA). Once while traveling, as the plane was landing, he noticed that the lady sitting next to him was extremely frightened by the plane's unstable descent. My friend is a very smart and creative young man, and he consequently designed a stabilization system for aircraft landing. For this magnificent invention with wide applications, he was given a $500 bonus by the FAA. Feeling that his talents were unappreciated and certainly not properly compensated, he decided to seek an engineering job in the private sector. On hearing about his experience with the FAA, his new employer assured him that if he came up with another great invention he would receive 20 percent of the profits.

Well, the young man did come up with another fabulous invention — one, in fact, that resulted in a $300 million profit for the company. To celebrate their success, the company held a ceremony, during which they were going to recognize my friend for his contribution. He invited his parents and many of his friends to be present when he would receive his check for $60 million. During the ceremony, the CEO of the company called him to the stage and presented him with a plaque and a glazed ham. The next day, the young man confronted the CEO in his office and asked about the $60 million. The CEO replied that it had been decided that they would invest that

$60 million in the further development of the company and that it would all be made right with him in the long run. My inventor friend tendered his resignation immediately and started to walk away when the CEO stopped him, walked over to his desk, and wrote a check for $75,000, which he handed to him. My friend tore up the check, threw it in the CEO's face, and walked out with the intention of starting his own company.

He quickly came to realize that his goal required significant capital, and that as a twenty-two-year-old black man with a bunch of ideas and very little collateral he was going to have a very difficult time realizing his dream. He went to ten different banks seeking a business loan and he was shut out on every occasion; however, he was offered an opportunity at each bank to receive a credit card with a $20,000 limit. He accepted all ten of the credit cards and used the credit of $200,000 to start his own engineering firm. As his inventive genius was given the opportunity it needed to succeed, his company grew and prospered, and he ultimately sold it for a nine-figure amount when he retired at age forty, which was his dream. Even though he is now extremely wealthy, he continues to work and engage in charitable endeavors to advance science and engineering education in America.

My friend's story of being taken advantage of is only one example of how greed can manifest itself within the capitalist system. Unfortunately, however, greed is a significant drawback for *any* economic model, including communism and socialism. No one can justify ascribing a flaw in human character to one economic model or another, for greed is a human weakness seen in all societies.

In the Bible, God instituted a system of tithing, which meant giving 10 percent of one's profits back to God. Since God is all powerful and owns everything, he certainly does not need any percentage of our profits. So why did he institute tithing? Could it be that he understood that all human beings are subject to greed and that by requiring them to give away 10 percent of their profits they might learn a valuable lesson about not hoarding and about voluntarily sharing with others?

UP THE ECONOMIC LADDER

As a member of the Horatio Alger Association of Distinguished Americans,[2] I could easily fill this entire book with others' inspiring rags-to-riches stories. If you think long and hard enough, you probably know someone yourself with a wonderful success story. My inventor friend worked very hard and part of his motivation was his own financial independence. But on the way to achieving financial independence, he created many jobs, and I know others who also became financially independent because of their association with this man's company. Sometimes the creation of jobs and the wealth that are side effects of someone else's efforts and creativity get labeled as "trickle-down economics," because inventing needed products creates jobs and opportunities for others and therefore should be encouraged if the aim is to have a prosperous society.

Many Americans understand this correlation between their own hard work and success, a cause-effect relationship that led to the can-do attitude that brought us to the economic table with the big boys of the world when we were still a fledgling nation barely fifty years old. As our country developed, so too did a sense of personal responsibility and pride in the ability to take care of oneself and one's family. People were willing to take menial jobs in order to support their families with the intention of increasing their knowledge and skills, thus increasing their value and eventually moving them up the economic ladder. There were a variety of economic outcomes for persons depending on their productivity and value to an organization or to their community. In other words, the harder you worked and the more value you produced, the higher you moved up the economic ladder of financial success.

Of course, there are many in our society who bring only entertainment value, and American society is as enamored with celebrity as British society is with royalty. Although I have nothing against sports and entertainment, I believe there is a danger of getting lost in a fantasy world while neglecting the serious things in life such as education and productive work. The enormous salaries paid to sports stars and entertainers lead people to believe that they are the most important people in our society, or have the most important jobs. I believe they are as important as anyone else, but we must ask ourselves what will maintain the pinnacle position of our nation in the world: the ability to shoot a twenty-five-foot jump shot, or the ability to solve a quadratic equation.

Capitalism is a system that works extremely well for someone who is highly motivated and very energetic, but it is not a great system for someone who is not interested in working hard or for someone who feels no need to contribute to the economic well-being of their community. People in the latter group frequently rationalize about their value to society and develop a sense of entitlement to the fruits of other people's labors. In fairness, I should add that some people work extremely hard and make significant contributions to society, yet choose low-paying careers or give away most of their resources to others. Such individuals form an important part of the capitalist model. For example, you are unlikely to meet any successful person who cannot point to a teacher who played a significant, positive role in their development. In some cases it is a minister, priest, rabbi, or other spiritual mentor. Many such individuals choose a life not overflowing with material things, because they receive incalculable non-tangible rewards through the work they choose.

However, the important word here is *choose*, since these people have a choice, understand the consequences of those choices, and are at peace with their decisions.

THE FREEDOM OF CHOICE

I had to make a very critical choice toward the end of my neurosurgical residency, deciding whether to stay in academic medicine or go into private practice where I would earn substantially more money. Having grown up in poverty, I felt drawn toward private practice and the dream of financial independence. At the same time, I felt that I could make a contribution to medicine if I became a full-time academic neurosurgeon at Johns Hopkins. After prayerful consideration, I chose the academic route, but after one and a half years, I was beginning to think I had made the wrong choice, because I was working very hard, fourteen to sixteen hours every day, doing a tremendous number of very stressful neurosurgical procedures, involving myself in several research endeavors, and making only $75,000 a year. I understand that to many readers that will seem like an enormous amount of money, but it really is a relatively meager salary for a fully trained neurosurgeon, even in an academic practice, who still has to pay off high medical school loans.

So I decided to join a private neurosurgical practice in Texas, which was going to pay me six times more than I was making at Hopkins. When I submitted my letter of resignation, it was not accepted and the powers that be convinced me that I was being hasty in my decision. They said that all of my grievances could easily be remedied and that a new salary incentive program was being implemented. I poured out my heart to God before I made the decision, trying to justify my reasons for leaving. But I felt strongly that I should stay and believed that I would be treated fairly and properly compensated for my work.

Ultimately I did decide to stay, and it turned out I could never have had the career that I've had if I had gone into private practice. Shortly thereafter I gained a great amount of international notoriety, which led to the writing of my first book, *Gifted Hands*, which has sold more than one million copies. I became a popular and well-compensated public speaker, and I was invited to sit on Fortune 500 corporate boards. The salary incentive program at Hopkins worked very well too. All of this put me in a much stronger financial position than if I had gone into private practice.

Using my God-given talents, listening to my heart, and working very hard in a capitalistic economy certainly paid large dividends for me. My wife, Candy, and I were able to realize our dream of starting a national scholarship program for children of all backgrounds, with the goal of inspiring a new generation of incredibly bright, ethical leaders to take the reins of our nation. I make no apologies for the fact that I am considered one of the rich in this nation, but I am proud of the fact that our single largest annual expense (excluding taxes) is charitable contributions, and I happen to know that that is the case with many of our personal friends who are also well-to-do.

Choice is vitally important in the capitalist economic model, for people must have the freedom to choose not only what they want to do, but how much effort they want to put into their work. It is truly a wonderful feeling to be able to voluntarily help someone who has financial needs, which they are trying unsuccessfully to resolve. It is considerably less pleasant to be forced to give your hard-earned resources to others regardless of their circumstances. Americans traditionally have been the most generous people in the world, and we should recognize and celebrate that rather than extinguish such a wonderful trait with unfair taxation. Not only should we be concerned about unfair taxation, but we also need to recognize the deleterious effect of unfair business practices and overregulation.

THE EARLY BIRD GETS THE WORM

When I was in college, one of my summer jobs was supervisor for highway cleanup crews. I directed groups of young men who picked up debris along the highway with huge plastic bags. It was quite a difficult job because the weather was so hot and there was very little shade along the expressway. Needless to say, the guys weren't all that enthusiastic about the job. As the supervisor, I wanted us to do a good job, so I began to think of ways to give them incentives.

"You guys don't really want to be picking up garbage in the hot sun, do you?" I asked one day after gathering them together.

"You got that right!" they shouted.

Then I said, "Why don't we start when it's cool out? How about six in the morning?"

"Six in the morning?" they shot back. "You must be crazy. What are they teaching you at that fancy school?"

I then went on to explain that they could work much more efficiently during the cool weather, and that I would pay them for eight hours of work if they could fill a hundred bags with garbage in seven or even six hours. Whatever amount of time it took, I would still pay them for eight hours if they accomplished the task. Well, you have never seen people work like these young men worked from that point on. By eight o'clock in the morning they would have filled more than two hundred bags with garbage and cleaned whole stretches of highway.

Those in charge of the program were flabbergasted. They were always saying, "Carson's crews are amazing, but we never see them."

This, to a large extent, is what the capitalistic economic model is based on. Giving incentives to work hard not only worked for them, it works for society at large. Now, I could not give the men the rest of the day off because they had to punch timecards, but as a result of their hard work, I was able to allow them to have leisurely days with extended lunch breaks and walks in the park. If I'd had the authority to pay them more money for more work, they would have been happy to continue working to make more money. Without any incentives for productivity (capitalistic model), they were quite content do nothing, which unfortunately is the by-product of any system that bases wages solely on head counts (socialistic model).

THE PARABLE OF THE WORKERS

There is definitely room to argue about whether the fruits of one's labors should be equally distributed throughout the society or whether one should be able to directly benefit from working harder than others around him. When I was an eight-year-old boy living in Boston, I had an opportunity to earn a whole dollar and a delicious-looking candy bar with nuts and caramel in exchange for shelling several bushels of peas for a neighbor who had just purchased them from the farmers' market. Six of us agreed, and all we had to do was sit in the kitchen and shell peas. Although it was more fun to be outside playing, we didn't have to sit in the hot sun and we could talk while we did the work, so it wasn't as much of a chore as it could have been. The idea of earning money and getting a nice-sized candy bar to boot was more than enough incentive for us to agree. Four of us worked extremely hard all day while two boys did virtually nothing. I was among the hard workers and at the end of the day, when the rewards were handed out, I was somewhat dismayed to see that everyone received the same compensation. The four boys who did all the work protested, but the two other boys claimed that they had done just as much, and they prevailed.

Some would say that there is a parable in the Bible that supports the two boys who did nothing, found in Matthew 20:1–16. In this parable focusing on grace, a land owner hires workers to work in his vineyard, agreeing to pay them a certain sum for a day's labor. In the last hour of the working day, he hires more workers and at the end of the day pays them the same as the ones who had been working all day. The early workers are disgruntled and feel that they have been treated unfairly, but the landowner accurately points out that they had been paid the wage that was agreed upon; therefore, nothing unjust had been done to them. Furthermore, he makes the point that he has the right to do with his own money as he pleases.

This parable seems to score points for both sides, because on the one hand it advocates equal pay for everyone regardless of how much work was done by any particular person, and on the other hand it argues for the sovereignty of the landowner, who should be able to use his money any way he wants. Many capitalists would side with the early workers, while many socialists would side with the late workers, but I think the point of the parable is that you should do your own work in a responsible manner, be satisfied if you are paid according to the agreed amount, and not worry about what someone else is getting.

Each of the early workers also had the knowledge and reassurance that they would have a full day's worth of remuneration that day and could afford to feed their families. The workers who arrived later in the day would have experienced more angst and stress in their search for work until they met up with the generous landowner. The landowner, by offering the various jobs, enabled each of the workers to experience a sense of accomplishment that they were able to provide for themselves and their families through their own efforts. The landowner could have decided to hold on to his money and spend it on something else, or place it somewhere safe (away from tax revenue collectors), rather than expanding his business.

It only complicates your life when you begin to worry about what everybody else is doing and how much everyone else has. An overreaching government might decide in this case to confiscate much of the money of the land owner and redistribute it in a more equitable fashion, at least according to its value system. Then again, if the government did not interfere, the early industrious workers would soon learn how to negotiate a better contract, since the land owner clearly had plenty of money and needed a lot of work to be done. This is how capitalism works, assuming that people are able to make decisions for themselves in their own best interests.

Let the Reward Fit the Performance

The seeds of capitalism are sown early during the educational process in this country during which young people are rewarded for superior academic performance with high grades, ribbons, medals, and various other types of recognition. They begin to develop the mind-set of winners and a can-do attitude, which is essential for success in the capitalist model. Some school districts today discourage differentiating students based on academic performance because they feel that it makes the students who do not achieve as well feel inferior. And some people feel that all teachers should also be treated the same and that it is inappropriate to reward superior teachers or to penalize inferior teachers. Such a system, however, seldom produces outstanding teachers or outstanding students. If mediocrity becomes the norm, the quantity of outstanding producers will decline, as will general prosperity.

Children are especially vulnerable to peer pressure, whether it be good peer pressure or bad peer pressure. It is definitely possible to affirm students who are not doing as well academically while still providing encouraging extra recognition for those students who are achieving the highest levels. By providing extra recognition for those outstanding students, many of the other students are encouraged to try harder. We have certainly found this to be the case with the Carson Scholars Fund, which provides scholarships for students who demonstrate both superior academic performance and humanitarian qualities. Some teachers have told us that when we put a Carson scholar in the classroom, the grade-point average of the whole class can go up by as much as one point over the next year.

When students embrace the concept of striving for excellence, it completely changes their opinion of who they are and what they can do. It did for me. Jaime Escalante was the subject of *Stand and Deliver*, a movie depicting his life as a teacher in the inner city, where the prevailing attitude was that calculus was way beyond the students' capabilities. By getting to know those students individually and working with them, he was able to convince more and more of them that they were smart—after that, teaching them calculus was a piece of cake. During his tenure, that school had more advanced placement calculus students than all but three other public high schools in the country.[3]

The concept of rewards for production lies at the foundation of capitalism and needs to be understood. The anticipation of rewards for being productive and the fear of consequences for being unproductive are great human motivators for both young and old. Historically, when these motivators are removed, productivity declines. Nonproductive people frequently make excuses for their lack of production, and as long as they can utilize those excuses, they have no reason to change their ways. But motivate them and watch what happens.

For example, if you met someone living on the streets who had no house, no car, and very little if any money, and you were able to convince him that if he met you in Bismarck, North Dakota, in seventy-two hours that you would give him $1 million, I can virtually assure you that he would find a way to get there. People can generally find a way to do what they want to do, and they can find a hundred excuses for what they don't want to do. When you have an entire society of people with a great work ethic and a sense of personal responsibility, that society will take off like a rocket and quickly achieve a position of power and leadership. I give you the United States of America.

Some people with a socialist agenda claim that the Bible supports their system of government because the early Christians pooled their resources and because Jesus lived like a peasant. Having read the Bible in its entirety several times, that's not my conclusion. The early Christians had a dramatic mission to accomplish in a relatively short period of time, and without using their collective talents and resources, it would have been extraordinarily difficult to have had the impact on the whole world as quickly as they did. Also, since the vast majority of people were workers and peasants, it is likely that Jesus reasoned that his greatest impact would be among the largest segment of society, and that he was much more likely to reach them as a worker himself. Besides, great characters of the Bible such as Job, King David, King Solomon, Lot, and Abraham were people of extraordinary wealth and influence, and they became heroic figures and men of God, so that point had already been made.

In the parable of the talents,[4] in fact, industry and concerted effort are praised while laziness is rejected. For those who are not familiar with this story, a master had three servants, and as he was departing for a long journey, he gave each of them a certain number of talents.[5] The first servant was given five bags of money, which through his efforts he managed to double. The second servant was given two bags of money, which he managed to double also, while the third servant was given only one bag of money, which he buried in the ground, hoping to conserve it. When the master returned, he was very pleased with the efforts of the first and second servants and concluded that they were worthy of even more rewards since through their stewardship they had managed to produce even more than he had originally given them. When the third servant was asked what had become of the talent that he was given, he said to the master, "I know that you are a harsh taskmaster, therefore I buried the talent to ensure that nothing happened to it and that I would not diminish your gift." The master was extremely angry with the servant and commanded that his talent be given to the one who had multiplied his talents the most.

This parable is remarkable in that it shows God encourages the same kind of traits that lead to entrepreneurship and business success. Being lazy and content with the status quo is shunned, while being highly industrious is praised. Since this parable was told by Jesus himself, it gives us some insight into how those who believe in the Bible and in the teachings of Christ should view the positive aspects of capitalism. You will notice that I said "the *positive* aspects of capitalism," which suggests there are negative aspects as well. We have discussed greed already, which really encompasses most of the other negative aspects of capitalism, such as lack of regard for the environment.

Many of the industrialists who helped propel our country to the forefront of the global economy were much more interested in growing their businesses than they were in protecting the environment. The result? Dangerous pollution and the compromised habitat of many animals. Protecting the environment is neither a Democratic nor a Republican position, but rather it should be a *logical* position for capitalists *and* socialists, because everyone should be looking out for the interests of future generations and trying to protect their own health as well. Having a clean and healthy environment is beneficial to everyone no matter what their political persuasion. If our government were able to identify what needs to be done in our country to protect our environment, and our representatives (who are supposed to be looking out for their constituents) agreed on our policies and followed through on them, it would benefit us all.

TO WHOM MUCH IS GIVEN ...

I once met legendary entrepreneur A. G. Gaston,[6] a multimillionaire who had funded a significant portion of the civil rights movement in the South. He was ninety-five years old at the time, and during our conversation together at Tuskegee University in Alabama, I asked him the following question: "Mr. Gaston, how did you as a black man become a multimillionaire in Birmingham, Alabama, in the 1930s to 1950s?" For as most of you will know, Birmingham, Alabama, was a bastion of racism during that time.

"It's very simple," he said. "I just opened my eyes, looked around, and asked myself, what do people need? I then went about fulfilling those needs."

In the process, he created multiple businesses, including an insurance company and a bank, and in doing so he became a very wealthy individual. But it was what he did with that wealth that was extraordinary—supporting the civil rights struggles in Birmingham and throughout the South. This is a splendid example of a capitalist who was extraordinarily compassionate and did a great deal to improve society for all of us.

Many like-minded capitalists make enormous contributions to the well-being of our society. Sometimes contributions are made on a smaller scale than that of Gaston, but all of these contributions, large or small, add up. Hundreds of thousands of bright, hard-working entrepreneurs start their own businesses to ensure their own financial security and the security of their families. In the process they create jobs for other people. In fact, small businesses create 80 percent of the private sector jobs in this country. In 2010, before the national elections, the question of whether or not to raise taxes on the "rich" (defined by the government as families with a household income of $250,000 a year or more) was widely debated. Some felt that anyone making that much money could certainly afford to pay more taxes, and in fact should do so since the vast majority of the population did not enjoy such affluence. Wealth should be redistributed fairly, they argued.

However, those who were targeted for this tax increase included many small business owners. And those with a better understanding of how capitalism works felt just as strongly that it would be a huge mistake to impose higher taxes on the very people who create the majority of private sector jobs. If you continually punish those who are economically successful through higher and higher taxes, at some point you extinguish the desire to work hard, since they will be working harder for a smaller return and their profits will increasingly go to the government. Many of the rich people in this country have been extremely generous with their money, and they are to be commended for this generosity. Some haven't. But the government shouldn't take from either of them against their will. The Constitution is quite clear that the government has the right to tax in order to support its programs, but there is nothing in the Constitution to support redistribution of wealth. Some proponents of big government get around this by creating many programs and then argue that these have to be supported by taxes. In this way they redistribute wealth according to their agenda. As a society we need to be mature enough to recognize that the wealthy in this nation provide many opportunities for those who are not rich by creating jobs and paying taxes. The fact is, the top 50 percent of wage earners in the United States pay 97 percent of the taxes. The top 2 percent earn 19 percent of all wages, but pay

52 percent of all taxes. Since almost 50 percent of the population pays no federal income tax at all, you can see that the more affluent constituents of society are already supporting the less fortunate to a large extent.

I am a huge proponent of humanitarian efforts, and I strongly believe that "[to whom] much is given, of him shall be much required" (Luke 12:48). This is the reason that the humanitarian component of the Carson Scholars Fund is so important. In order to be nominated for one of the scholarships, a student must not only have a near-perfect grade point average, but he or she must also demonstrate humanitarian qualities. A student cannot win if they are simply smart and successful, but don't care about other people, for we want to encourage the same values of productivity and generosity that characterize many of the men and women who helped this nation become the world power that it is today.

CAPITALISM HAS WORKED WELL— AND IT COULD WORK AGAIN

Capitalism has worked very well for the United States of America, but like every economic system it does have its shortcomings. There is no perfect system quite simply because there are no perfect people. Even with capitalism, some government regulation is necessary. As James Madison said, "If men were angels, no government would be necessary."[7]

As I mentioned earlier in this chapter, it is true that some capitalists care only about making money and disregard the well-being of their fellow human beings and the environment. A responsible government certainly should exercise oversight in every economic model—including the capitalist model. Appropriate regulations should protect the environment and the rights of all its citizens. For example, a chemical factory should not be allowed to dump toxic waste in an area where people or significant animal populations can be harmed. By the same token, some degree of government regulation is necessary for our large financial institutions to prevent the kinds of tragedies that occurred during and immediately after the great stock market crash of 1929 and again in 2008. The real shame is that we did recognize the importance of financial regulation after the great crash of 1929 and appropriately developed safeguards in the 1930s. Unfortunately, we decided to deregulate during the 1990s, paving the way for the economic meltdown in 2008.

When it comes to defending the economic viability of our nation, it is naïve to count on the honesty and integrity of people responsible for our markets when they stand to gain so much by manipulating the system to their advantage. If we become paranoid and overregulate the financial markets, however, we will not see peak performance from them. That hurts everybody's retirement plans with its domino effects. This is one of the reasons that a balance of viewpoints in our legislative bodies is not only healthy but also necessary. Our founding fathers understood human nature, including the desire for power and a tendency toward greed; therefore, our broad regulatory principles should be aimed at stifling excessive power and greed. We need many wise counselors focusing on the kinds of regulations that accomplish these goals without suppressing productivity and growth.

With all of the intellect that exists in our nation, it should be easy for us to come up with bipartisan, business-friendly policies to encourage businesses and manufacturers to bring their factories and offices back to our land. Logical people from both political parties should sit down with business leaders who have moved much of their business offshore and ask them why they did, then work with them to find solutions that will bring them back. We all want a prosperous and thriving nation, and if we appropriately analyze the problems that preclude prosperity, we can certainly find the solutions.

Doing so would lead to the creation of jobs, which is essential to the maintenance of the middle class, the backbone of America. A friend of mine who lives in Connecticut is a self-made multimillionaire who owns many businesses and has a very keen business mind. In order to instantly create many more jobs in the United States, he has proposed that we place a stiff tariff on products that are manufactured in other countries and are shipped here fully assembled, while reducing tariffs on products that will require assembly once they reach our shores. In order to assemble the latter group of products, many workers would have to be hired. Given the severe trade imbalance that we already are experiencing, such a policy would have a dramatic impact on the American job market. This is just one example of how government could enhance job creation, thus expanding the tax base rather than killing jobs with ever-increasing taxes.

Today we live in the information age where knowledge is power, yet—as I discussed earlier—almost one third of all our students drop out of high school before graduation.[8] In many inner-city schools the dropout rate is considerably higher than that. It is time for corporate America and the rest of society to band together to stop the hemorrhaging and give these young people the incentive and tools to complete their education and become a part of a "can-do" society versus a "what can you do for me" society. For a well-functioning capitalistic society cannot sustain itself without a steady supply of enthusiastic and hard-working individuals who are excited about achieving the American dream.

—CHAPTER 6—

SOCIALISM: WHOSE POT OF SOUP IS IT?

SINCE MY MOTHER had only a third-grade education and was functionally illiterate, there weren't many lucrative job opportunities available to her. To compensate, she worked two and sometimes even three jobs, cleaning the houses of wealthy families and caring for their children. She frequently left the house at five in the morning and did not return until midnight, which meant that Curtis and I would sometimes not see her for several days at a time. When she was at home, you could see the fatigue in her eyes, but the little time and energy she did have, she always spent on Curtis and me. It was clear that whether she was working or spending time with us, she wanted us to have a better life than the one we had.

When other families went on outings, for example, we couldn't. There simply wasn't enough money. Every once in a while, however, Mother would save up enough for us to go to the fair, but only enough for us to get in the gate — we had to enjoy the rides by watching others. We couldn't try our hand at any of the games, no matter how much we practiced pitching coins or playing basketball at home. Most adults can recall wonderful childhood tastes from nibbling on cotton candy, hot dogs, french fries, ice cream, and rainbow-colored snow cones, but Curtis and I had to be content to only smell — never taste.

Being unable to give us many of the little joys of childhood weighed heavily on Mother. When we'd arrive at the checkout counter in a grocery store and have to run the inevitable gauntlet of assorted candies, we'd ask her if we could have something "this time," but the answer was always no. The look in her eyes was so devastating that after a while we wouldn't even ask. There was no money for a babysitter either, so Curtis and I were pretty much left on our own.

But Mother was always creative in coming up with ways for us to make ends meet. In the summertime, for example, when farmers' crops were ready for harvest, she would drive us out to the country on the weekend, stop at a farmhouse, and offer to pick four bushels of a crop if we could keep one. Farmers usually complied, and we'd bring home fresh vegetables or fruit, such as strawberries, peaches, tomatoes, and green beans. Although we may have complained about the work, it was fun picking produce together as a family. And once we returned home, she would can many of the items to sustain us during the winter months.

Most of Mother's friends and relatives also struggling with economic hardship were quite happy to lean on public assistance. As a child, I overheard many conversations in which they detailed schemes — some of which were quite elaborate — for obtaining more government aid. *Take a course in a community college,* I heard them say, *to make it appear that you are trying to escape welfare. That will get you extra money for child care. Your social worker, who will be so happy and proud of you, can be easily manipulated. By the time they grow weary of their work and move on, another one will have been assigned to your case.* I often wonder what they could have accomplished if they had spent that intellectual energy developing a new business. My mother steadfastly resisted her friends' lifestyle because, even though she only had a third-grade education, she had noticed that almost no one who became a welfare mom ever came off of welfare, and she was repulsed by the thought of perpetually depending on others.

The attitude of my mother's friends and relatives was very similar to that of the students in a course I took in school, in which only two grades were given: *satisfactory* and *unsatisfactory.* Many of the students in that particular class — who usually strove to excel — relaxed and set aside any notion of spending long hours studying to get an *A* on an exam, let alone working for extra credit. After all, they knew they would receive at best a grade of *satisfactory* no matter how hard they worked. On the one hand, it comforted many students to know that they would pass the course without ever having to extend themselves much — but on the other hand, it discouraged many students from working hard to achieve excellence.

Some might question the wisdom of my mother's drive toward self-sufficiency and her no-nonsense parenting of us boys, but I believe the proof is in the pudding: one son became an aviation engineer and the other became a neurosurgeon, two of the most prestigious professions. Many children of the wealthy clients for whom she worked managed to only just get by in life or worse—some ended up dead, in the penal system, or on welfare.

My journey from inner-city poverty to board-certified neurosurgeon was arduous and expensive, as it is for anyone who decides to become a doctor. Today, even those from middle-class families graduate from medical school with student debt equivalent to the mortgage on a house. They are not able to pay off those debts for several more years because they also have to complete an internship—and, in many cases, several years of residency with very modest wages. Doctors today are frequently well into their thirties by the time they are able to even begin addressing their debts. In many other countries, medical education is completely subsidized by the government, because they realize that the physicians will contribute substantially to the well-being of their society. Since the graduating doctors in those countries are not saddled with the burden of great financial debt, they are free to choose the area of medicine that appeals most to them without focusing on the salary of any given specialty.

The question then is, are there aspects of socialism that are worth keeping or incorporating into the fabric of our society? Or does capitalism have the upper hand when it comes to solutions?

RISKS AND REWARDS

In the United States, physicians in high-paying specialties are increasing much faster than primary care physicians, largely because graduating doctors choose their specialties based on the amount of debt they have incurred rather than based on their interests and talents. This is a problem that we can solve quickly and relatively inexpensively by eliminating or greatly reducing medical school tuition. By embracing a positive aspect of socialism, medical education would be subsidized for the good of the entire nation. Admitting there are beneficial aspects of socialism, however, does not obligate us to completely reorient our nation's economic system. The resulting increase in the number of primary care physicians would address many of the problems that patients in this country currently face regarding access to doctors.

However, in the same way that capitalists and socialists differ over who should pay for and receive benefits, tension exists in the medical community over the disparity in salaries among the specialties. Those in the lower-paying specialties frequently resent what they consider excessive salaries paid to specialists such as cardiothoracic surgeons and neurosurgeons. In multispecialty practices or academic medical centers, those lucrative specialty departments usually subsidize the other departments, making things more equitable. I bring this up because this paradigm reflects our society at large and is somewhat analogous to the argument between capitalism and socialism. Capitalists would say that those who work the longest and hardest, and are exposed to the most risk, should receive the greatest financial rewards, while socialists would say that everyone has essentially equal training and the same general profession, thus it is unfair for one to receive more compensation than another.

It is easy to see validity in both points of view upon a superficial analysis; however, a deeper look at the differences between the specialties is revealing. Certain specialties, such as neurosurgery and obstetrics, face enormous medico-legal costs because we continue to leave tort reform — legal reform aimed at reigning in out-of-control lawsuits within the health-care sector — unaddressed. In some of our major cities such as Philadelphia and Chicago, the average malpractice premium for a neurosurgeon exceeds $300,000 annually. It is also commonly accepted that the three most stressful occupations are 911 operator, air traffic controller, and neurosurgeon. Neurosurgeons generally die several years earlier than the population at large. I recently went back and calculated the average age of death of ten neurosurgeons that I knew personally and was shocked to discover the number to be in the lower sixties. I'm hopeful that that age is now on the rise since more attention is being placed on the number of hours worked and alleviation of stress, but we still have a long way to go. Many people in surgical specialties also have to retire earlier because physical skills decline more quickly than mental skills. Although many wish to deny it, vision and dexterity at age seventy is unlikely to be comparable to the same at age thirty. So when one takes into account years of training, amount of stress, life expectancy, and earlier retirement, it should be easy to see that few people would consider certain specialties if there were no differential remuneration. This is not to say that these individuals are only interested in money, but in a capitalistic society, risk taking and sacrifice are frequently rewarded financially.

WHICH WAY ARE IMMIGRANTS FLOWING?

Not long ago, Candy and I had an opportunity to visit Cuba with a group of young American business leaders. There the government essentially owns and controls everything, including where people live, what they do for a living, and how much they earn. Certain people who are smiled on by the government are allowed to rent elegant accommodations and enjoy a privileged lifestyle, while the vast majority of the population must be satisfied with meager resources. However, their basic health-care needs are taken care of and they are unlikely to be homeless or starving.

A university professor in Cuba makes little more than an unskilled laborer—and in some cases less. In addition, many of our waiters and waitresses had advanced education degrees, but found that they could earn more money waiting tables. The many street vendors and performers in the main city squares created a festive façade, but having spoken to many Cuban refugees, I could only sympathize with the masses of people and hope that someday they can experience true freedom. Although some people, such as the documentary filmmaker Michael Moore, extol the virtues of Cuban society, the tide of illegal immigration is from Cuba to America, not vice versa. More people seem to prefer freedom with the opportunity to create security than security without freedom. If people could freely choose which type of society they preferred to live in, life would be very fair. Unfortunately, although Americans are free to leave this country any time they want to go live somewhere else, such privileges are not afforded to the average Cuban or those in many other countries where the government controls their lives.

IN SOCIALISM, SOME ARE STILL MORE EQUAL THAN OTHERS

To be fair, some people love socialism's ideas, which they see as bringing about a utopian existence. They feel there is less conflict and competition when everyone is treated the same. But does the socialist ideal of equality hold?

One summer, I worked at a Chrysler plant in Detroit as a preassembly line worker, monotonously welding hour after hour. It was quite boring work, and I received a decent salary whether I worked hard or decreased my production. What I really wanted to do was be a driver who moved the finished product from the end of the assembly line to a large parking lot. Those jobs went to a privileged few with connections in the company. However, I worked so hard at my job that eventually management noticed and gave me my dream job as a driver.

In socialistic systems, as in capitalist ones, intelligence and diligence are often eventually noticed, and individuals are moved into privileged positions. In other words, you could say that although everyone is equal in socialism, some are more equal than others. So differential treatment is a part of socialism just as it is in capitalism, but in the latter system, self-dependency and self-reliance play the larger role in one's advancement, whereas in the former system, currying favor with the powers that be and hoping to be noticed plays the larger role in advancement.

DOES SOCIALISM'S SAFETY NET HOLD OR EVENTUALLY TEAR UNDER THE WEIGHT?

One of the most appealing aspects of socialism is the safety net it provides for its citizens. Because all resources are supposedly distributed in an equitable fashion, there should be enough money, food, and services to provide everyone with a reasonable lifestyle. Theoretically, socialism eliminates the disparity between some living with great wealth while others live in poverty. This system requires that the government have intimate knowledge of everyone's personal property and resources in order to be able to redistribute wealth. Although most Americans have great compassion for those less fortunate than themselves, very few would agree to involuntarily sharing all they had earned by their hard work with people they didn't even know.

When I was growing up, a homeless man came to our church one Sabbath, and he kept talking about how hungry he was. My mother had made an enormous pot of chili, my favorite food, so she invited the man home for dinner. I have never seen anyone eat so many bowls of chili, but he was eventually satisfied, as was my mother. I saw many acts of kindness by my family and many others over the years, and I believe that generosity is part of the American way of life. However, I suspect that my mother would have been quite unhappy if a government agent had come along and confiscated her chili in order to share it with others who had nothing to eat. She would have felt that it was her chili, and that she had the right to share with whomsoever she wished. And therein lies one of the fundamental differences between capitalism and socialism.

Socialism's underlying goal of sharing with others is noble. But amazingly, many Americans who are having financial difficulty would reject the idea of the government confiscating the assets of the wealthy to balance things out. This attitude bewilders many who believe in "taxing the rich" and redistributing that wealth as the solution to everything. Many of those seeking to gain political advantage in our system recognize that there are far more poor people than there are rich people, and that by stirring up class warfare they can create an enormous power base for themselves. So far this political strategy has failed to yield the promised fruit because most Americans value freedom above financial security, just as centuries ago the colonists rejected the protection promised by the British Crown, coupled with its ever-increasing taxes.

As a testament to how socialism's safety net can begin to tear under the strain, in 2010, several financially distressed countries—Greece and Ireland as the prominent examples—experienced dramatic shortages of money, making it impossible for them to continue their overly generous social programs the general populace had come to expect. Massive protests and violent rioting broke out in the streets because people felt robbed of what they felt was their rightful share of the country's production. These countries had overextended themselves in terms of the benefits they had promised and simply could not take in enough revenue to fulfill their obligations. This unfortunately has happened in the past and will happen in the future because government-controlled programs continue to grow until they destroy themselves. The founding fathers of this nation were well aware of the perils associated with gigantic government programs, which is why they emphasized limited government and self-reliance. All you have to do is look at Greece and Ireland today to see the results of unrealistic promises made to the populace.

We can already see some of these socialist bubbles being popped here in our own nation. In the not too distant past, public service jobs in the United States usually paid less than private-sector jobs and didn't have as many benefits. It was indeed sacrificial public service. Today, government jobs pay on average 20 percent more than private-sector jobs of the same type and have mind-boggling benefits—all at the taxpayers' expense. Furthermore, if you have ever tried to deal with a government bureaucracy, you probably know how difficult it is to find caring and competent people. For many people, a government job is a ticket to an easy life. The founders of our nation intended for government workers to be representatives and servants of their communities rather than beneficiaries, and they never intended for public servants to be economically better off than the general populace. Such overcompensation places an enormous strain on government budgets, necessitating increased tax rates.

The desire to take care of everyone from cradle to grave is laudable, but I'm also pragmatic and realize that one can only take care of everyone until there's no more money, at which time one can take care of no one—or one can reduce the amount of financial aid and encourage people to live responsibly, to save, and to plan for the future. Obviously the latter option makes more sense in the long run. For some reason, in recent decades our national leaders have stopped looking so much at the long-term issues facing our country and have concentrated on short-term stopgap measures that temporarily make them look good politically.

The problem of caring for the indigent still remains, and as Jesus himself said, "The poor you will always have with you." Some are poor due to mental or physical illness and/or bad luck, and others are poor because they have no desire to work hard. There is a growing third group, however—those who work hard at lower-middle-class, blue-collar jobs, but whose salaries are unable to keep up with the inflation of a reckless government fiscal policy over the past few decades, resulting in real wages failing to keep up with the cost of living for a family. Should we make a distinction between these groups when doling out social benefits?

Believers in the capitalistic model are not likely to have a great deal of sympathy for those individuals who want to live off the labor of others, while believers in the socialistic model make provisions even for those individuals. I suspect, however, that if you took one hundred people and placed them in a capitalistic society for several months, you would find most of them gainfully employed a year later. If you took that same one hundred people and placed them in a socialistic society for several months, I suspect that a year later you would find a large number of them "on the dole." People tend to do what they need to do to survive and are unlikely to expend extra effort when it is unnecessary. This is the primary reason why traditionally socialistic societies are not highly productive.

HOW THEN SHALL WE LIVE?

There is no one-size-fits-all type of government, and much to the horror of some people, it is a fact that our own government is a blend of both capitalism and socialism. The issue, then, of how to handle able-bodied individuals who simply do not want to work in a society with mixed government, such as in the United States, remains very sticky. The issue can be demagogued endlessly by both sides without arriving at a solution. Approaching the issue logically, however, there are three practical solutions:

1. Tell those who don't work that they are on their own.
2. Take from those who have something and redistribute it to the individuals who aren't working.
3. Borrow from a third party in order to take care of the nonworking individuals and leave the debt to future generations.

Logically, with solution 1, the individual who isn't working clearly either starves or finds a job. What about solution 2? In this case, those who are forcibly constrained to support the individuals who aren't working eventually lose interest in working themselves, since the fruits of their labors are being confiscated. This, in turn, leads to even more individuals who aren't working. What about solution 3? The other party buys our treasury notes in great quantities, thereby acquiring ownership of a significant portion of our nation. But these investors are unlikely to extend credit indefinitely, nor will future generations continue to remain ignorant of this downward spiral forever. At some point, they will realize that their future is being compromised, and they will refuse to go along with the program. Thus solution 1 is the only one that stands the test of logic and is the one upon which we should concentrate.

Necessity is the mother of invention, and right now it is necessary for us to create jobs while providing incentives to entrepreneurs and CEOs to keep coming up with new innovations and products. We must realize that excessive pay for executives is demoralizing to workers who don't feel that someone else in the same organization is worth well over three hundred times more than they are.[1] Fortunately "say on pay" arrangements have entered corporate America recently, which allows shareholders to have a voice in compensation for top executives and makes boards of directors more careful in determining organizational compensation.

Is it possible to implement solution 1 in a compassionate fashion? Of course it is when compromise is introduced into the equation. Instead of immediately kicking individuals off the dole, they could be weaned off over the course of several months, giving them the opportunity to make necessary adjustments in their lives. Again I should point out that we are only talking about able-bodied individuals who are capable of working but simply refuse to do so. I doubt that anyone in America would raise serious objections to taking care of individuals who simply are not capable of caring for themselves. Unemployment benefits certainly can be a stopgap measure for those truly seeking employment, but temporarily out of work. They are, however, not a favor to many who are not truly seeking work, because the longer an unemployed individual is not working, the less employable he or she becomes. Such benefits should be linked to work that needs to be done in the community, such as Roosevelt's New Deal,[2] in which government programs were created to provide jobs and stimulate growth in industry, transportation, banking, housing, agriculture, and many other areas.

WHO DECIDES WHOSE HOUSE IT IS?
So what is the role of government when it comes to taking care of the poor? We can probably answer this question more easily if we leave off labels such as *capitalism* and *socialism*, and instead focus on principles. Government is

invested with power by the people, who are governed because it is much easier and more orderly to have a central authority than for each person to serve as an authority unto himself. Natural law dictates that people have a right to protect their lives and their property, and this is a concept with which there is general societal agreement across all types of governmental systems throughout the history of the world.

As an example, we live in a large country estate about thirty miles outside the city of Baltimore. Our kids are grown and have their own homes, and Candy and I are very content. We have no neighbors within shouting distance, and the drive from our front door to the public road is three quarters of a mile. If someone who lived nearby presented himself on our doorstep and demanded that we trade houses with him because he has a large family with many children and they need the space, whereas we have very few people and an extremely large house, I could refuse or I could voluntarily comply. If I refused and he became belligerent and attempted to forcibly evict us, I could attempt to protect my property, which could have some very unpleasant results, or I could call the police, which is an appropriate arm of our government, whose duty includes the protection of my property and my life. This is exactly what the founding fathers envisioned as one of our governmental functions. If, on the other hand, our government officials decided my house was too big and the neighbor's house too small for his large family, and that they should confiscate my house and give it to my neighbor—or at the very least tax me at a high enough rate that they could redistribute money to my neighbor, who could then buy a bigger house—that kind of intrusive government would exemplify the very thing our founding fathers tried to avoid.

Not only did Benjamin Franklin, Samuel Adams, and several of the other founding fathers speak out against government redistribution of property, but in 1795 the Supreme Court of the United States declared, "No man would become a member of a community in which he could not enjoy the fruits of his honest labor and industry. The preservation of property, then, is a primary object of the social compact.... The legislature, therefore, has no authority to make an act divesting one citizen of his freehold, and vesting it in another, without a just compensation. It is inconsistent with the principles of reason, justice and moral rectitude; it is incompatible with the comfort, peace and happiness of mankind; it is contrary to the principles of social alliance and every free government; and lastly, it is contrary to the letter and spirit of the Constitution."

In our attempt to be kind to the poor, we have deviated substantially from the principles involved in the founding of our nation. The United

States is, in fact, historically and currently the most philanthropic nation in the history of the world. But our founders fully realized that prolonged government-sponsored charity would destroy the values of hard work, self-reliance, and compassion.

I am involved with a number of charitable organizations that are dedicated to improving the lives of the many unfortunate people who live among us. One of those organizations is the Curtis D. Robinson Men's Health Institute at St. Francis Hospital and Medical Center in Hartford, Connecticut. The driving force behind this organization—which screens hundreds of men without medical insurance for prostate cancer, and offers free treatment when cancer is found—is my friend Curtis D. Robinson, who traveled from Alabama to Connecticut when he was sixteen years old and penniless. He was very industrious, worked extremely hard, became CEO and owner of various businesses, and is now a multimillionaire. He has given away seven-figure amounts, receiving nothing in return except the satisfaction of knowing that lives that would have been lost are being saved. Many physicians, administrators, and caring citizens have joined Curtis in his efforts, as have I. It is very difficult to travel to any community in our nation and not find charitable organizations specifically created to aid the indigent citizens of that community.

Our government used to fully understand the role of private-sector charitable organizations in ameliorating the plight of the poor. This is why the government offered tax deductions and exemptions for churches and other charitable organizations. Today the government actually competes with many of these private-sector charities while still offering them tax deductions. How does this wasteful duplication benefit government or us, its citizens? Certainly by creating huge government entitlement programs, the size and power of the government increases dramatically. Before long, people generally depend on government for everything from food and shelter, to health care and education, to a comfortable retirement, instead of looking to government for the basic protection of life and property, as well as providing public roads and public safety.

I believe Benjamin Franklin was one of the wisest men to ever walk the face of the Earth. Was he a womanizer who enjoyed partying a bit too much? Probably! But he was a first-rate scholar, scientist, inventor, writer, and diplomat who was instrumental in the formation of our nation. He warned against inappropriate compassion, such as giving a drunk the wherewithal to buy liquor or smothering the human instinct to strive and excel by providing all basic necessities. I don't think you can say that he was selfish and simply wanted to preserve his wealth, because the same Benjamin Franklin offered to pay the British from his own bank account for their losses during the Boston Tea Party in order to spare the colonists severe retribution by the King.[3] Statements by Franklin and many of the other founders make it very clear that they were extremely opposed to the concept of wealth redistribution, which is a basic tenet of socialism.[4]

At an even more fundamental level, they were very much opposed to the concept of a large, intrusive central government, which they felt was really no different than the European monarchies they were trying to escape. Consider the United States' rapid acceleration to pinnacle status by means of a system rewarding hard work and vigorously protecting individual assets while encouraging compassion and charity—why would we want to change unless there is historical proof that another system will work better?

In a socialist society, the government has the right to tax whomever it wishes for whatever amount it deems necessary, whenever it wants. This leads to abusive, unchecked power that can eventually deprive many of the people of their rights—as our Declaration of Independence states—to enjoy life, liberty, and the pursuit of happiness. The insidious nature of socialism, cloaked in a façade of compassion, makes it very dangerous to an uneducated and trusting populace. And as socialism creates dependency, it is well on its way to eliminating freedom of choice and incentives for high productivity and innovation.

UNIONS: STRANGLING THE GOOSE THAT LAID THE GOLDEN EGG

Stealth socialism has the ability to stay under the radar while co-opting legitimate entities such as unions, changing them into something that is barely recognizable. I have been a union member myself, and having grown up in Detroit, I am of course very familiar with the positive aspects of union representation.[5] In the early days of the Industrial Age, the advent of unions brought about the kind of collective bargaining that resulted in fair wages and reasonable working conditions. Benefits derived through unions helped create the most prolific middle class the world has ever seen. Unfortunately, with time, many of the union bosses began to concern themselves with power and influence, and used union dues (which had grown to become huge pots of money) to change the outcome of elections and to wreak havoc in many areas where money equaled power. By threatening strikes to further their causes, they were able to exact excessive wages and benefits from companies such as General Motors, Ford, and Chrysler, in the long run crippling these companies and rendering them noncompetitive. The union leaders, their lawyers, accountants, and administrators were not dumb people, and they were well aware of the position they were putting these companies in. Essentially they were strangling the goose that laid the golden egg. The blame for the recent downfall of Detroit's auto industry, however, does not rest solely on the shoulders of the union bosses. Top management in the auto industry negotiated deals that they knew were fiscally irresponsible and would be harmful to the company's future. They also knew that they would receive their golden parachutes—complete with multimillion-dollar severance packages for their irresponsibility—and be long gone when the day of reckoning arrived.

One of the themes you may have begun to notice is that those entities that are bad for our nation tend to want what they want now, without thought to how it will affect future generations. If you use that principle as a measuring stick, in most cases you can easily determine which unions and other entities are good and which are deleterious to the prosperity of our nation.

As this book is being written, massive protests are going on in the state of Wisconsin, where teachers' unions and state workers' unions are disgruntled about the governor's plan to bring the wildly out-of-control state budget back under control. One of the components of his plan involves having those workers make larger contributions to their own benefit packages rather than saddling taxpayers with that responsibility. Even with the increased amount of contribution, these workers will still be getting a much better and cheaper benefits package than their counterparts in the private sector. They realize this, and are therefore capitulating to that requirement. However, they are not willing to relent on the issue of decreased collective-bargaining rights. They feel that if they give on this point, the union will be weakened forever, and they will be at a significant disadvantage when negotiating for future benefits and rights. They do not want to be at a disadvantage when it comes to issues such as class size, tenure, and evaluation of teacher competency. Of course, none of these come under the traditional banner of collective bargaining. The union leaders are focused solely on what *they* want, and refuse to believe that the huge budget deficit is real. They believe the whole issue has been fabricated by the governor and his cronies in order to bring down the unions, but the accounting is fairly straightforward—Wisconsin is but one of many states in dire straits, facing enormous deficits in revenue. It is almost incomprehensible to me how selfish one must be to demand benefits today without consideration for what happens to our children tomorrow.

Nevertheless, I do not see those who disagree with me as enemies, and I am happy to engage them in conversations about our future and how to ensure success for our children.

CAPITALISM VS. SOCIALISM: CAN WE INCORPORATE THE BEST OF BOTH WORLDS?

The security provided by socialistic governments can be addicting to the point that citizens are willing to give up many of their individual rights. Although you have the right to accumulate wealth, there is not much incentive to do so if it can be confiscated by the government at will. Although you have the right to work many years beyond the traditional age of retirement, many who are addicted to the socialist system retire as early as possible. In many European countries, citizens often take advantage of this while they are in their fifties. As a result, those societies lose some of their most experienced and effective workers (and potential mentors), who do not want to miss out on overly generous retirement benefits guaranteed to them by a bloated government. When government interferes too much in the private lives of its citizens, the losses can become widespread.

In the previous chapter, we examined the enormous benefits to our country and to the world of an economic system (capitalism) that encourages innovation, hard work, and entrepreneurship. Now, after examining the pros and cons of socialism, we have seen mostly negative effects, even in terms of its lauded compassionate components, which seem good at first glance, but reveal disincentives to work and fiscal irresponsibility in the long run. Because we live in a free and open society, those who advocate socialism are free to do so, but for the well-read individual, it is easy to discern the agenda of the socialists and how they are implementing that agenda in an attempt to bring fundamental change to America.[6] The agenda? Total government control. For jobs, income, you name it. Anytime you give to government the responsibility and authority to provide government-made jobs, old-age financial security, "free" health care, and "free" education and indoctrination of children, it will control the lives of the people who live under its jurisdiction, and individual liberty and freedom of choice are sacrificed.

Sure, there are several different brands of socialism—at least as many types as there are would-be people-planners who wish to impose their plans to control the moral and economic lives of other people. But are you willing to surrender your precious liberties to a socialist state which promises "security" for everyone and government-enforced equality? Isn't this what

Hitler and other socialists promised the German people in his Nazi (national socialist) platform — a country in which government guarantees security and "equality" in exchange for giving up individual freedom? Will Americans fall for the same scam?

Since Americans are by nature individualistic and entrepreneurial, by definition, then, the socialist program is anti-American, to say nothing of totalitarian.

Socialism is an old dream. Some dreams are nightmares when put into practice.

It is possible, however, to extract socialism's positive aspects and actually implement them within capitalism. For example, providing basic health care for every citizen can be done quite easily without increasing our national debt one penny. If we address our inefficient and wasteful billing and collections procedures, move to a national electronic medical record, provide people with incentives to use clinics instead of emergency rooms for primary care, and engage in meaningful tort reform to limit costly lawsuits, we would have plenty of money to provide basic health care to all citizens of this country. We could also realize significant revenue by combating fraud in government entitlements such as Medicare and Medicaid. And in our free society, individuals wanting to purchase additional health-care insurance could certainly do so without negatively impacting anyone else.

Social Security, Medicare, Medicaid, and our food stamp program, among others, are all socialist-leaning programs that help provide our nation with a social safety net. Their growth, however, must be controlled, and self-sufficiency must be the goal of our society. The masses should not depend solely upon these social programs; instead, they should be encouraged early in life to make provisions for themselves and their families well into the future.

If we steadfastly resist the excessive growth of government and its ever-increasing appetite for tax money, reminding our government that there is a document known as the Constitution of the United States that defines and limits its role in our lives, then we will have an opportunity to learn from past mistakes and build on successes to create the kind of nation that will continue to work for all of us.

—CHAPTER 7—

WHAT IS A MORAL NATION?

I'VE ALWAYS BEEN A COMPASSIONATE PERSON—sometimes to a fault. After finishing high school and while pursuing my goal of becoming a physician, I befriended a young man whose personal troubles were interfering with his studies, putting him in grave danger of flunking out if he failed to pass the final comprehensive exam. Since his mind was so confused with all that was going on in his life at the time, he had been incapable of retaining material and had no chance of passing. Knowing me to be a very honest person with a deep relationship with God and a strong moral code of ethics, he was terrified to ask me what he felt was his only remaining choice: he wanted me to allow him to copy my answers.

This presented me with a great moral dilemma, because he was a good person who was normally quite capable of passing the exam; I knew that once he got through his personal problems, he would be fine. I tried hard to justify my involvement in cheating, and in the end I did indeed allow him to look at my answers, even though I knew it was wrong. He passed the exam with my help and went on to become a very successful professional who has made a positive difference in the lives of hundreds, if not thousands of people.

In this case, did the end justify the means? He had already gone to the administration requesting a leave of absence and was told that his only option was to pass the exam. Nevertheless, if he had exerted enough effort, I feel confident that another solution could have been found. I regret cheating, but I am profoundly happy for his success today.

Not long after that, when I was a psychology major delving into the mysteries of the human mind, I stepped unknowingly into yet another moral dilemma. During my research for one of the papers in an advanced psychology course, I found some passages that seemed particularly appropriate, and I included them in my writing. I did not, however, indicate that this was the work of someone else; frankly, I had never even heard of the term *plagiarism*.

When the professor asked me to make an appointment to discuss my paper, I was befuddled. When I stepped into his office, however, I could immediately sense the weight of the moment. He pointed out that I had plagiarized and told me that the consequences for doing so normally included expulsion. I could see all of my dreams of becoming a doctor dashed by my stupidity. Even though I did not know the implications of plagiarism, I certainly should have known inherently that what I was doing was wrong. I had done it before without consequences and probably would have continued doing it if I had not been caught. Fortunately for me, the professor was very compassionate, realized that I was naïve, and gave me a chance to rewrite the paper.

This raises another question: Is ignorance an acceptable excuse for unethical behavior? Certainly those who sanctioned slavery in America thought that black people were inferior and that they were actually doing them a favor by liberating them from the jungles of Africa to associate with "superior beings." How easy it is to suppress morality for the sake of expediency. They tried every form of rationalization to justify something that they knew was immoral and totally opposed to the self-evident truths that were part of the founding of this nation, namely that "all men are created equal."

But even that phrase raises questions about equality and how we treat our fellow man. When I was a medical student in Michigan, many of our clinical rotations took place at the county hospital, and a large number of the patients served at this facility were indigent and had no means of paying the hospital bills. Those patients were assigned to the service controlled by the chief resident—not yet an attending physician—while the patients with insurance were assigned to one of the attending physicians with more experience. The chief resident could consult with any attending physician about cases on his service, but he would be the primary caregiver. This meant that there was a double standard of care quality based on a patient's ability to pay. This practice was common throughout the nation at that time, but has now been largely abandoned. One could legitimately argue that charity cases should be grateful for whatever they can get and that there is nothing immoral about differentiating the care that people receive based on status.

As a society, we make life-and-death decisions all the time based on status. When a disaster occurs, we evacuate children and women first. If a boat is sinking, the lifejackets go to the most vulnerable passengers. This greatly complicates the task of deciding what is or is not moral. In the case of the patients at the county hospital, they all received excellent care, and the majority of them did not even realize that their primary caregiver was a resident rather than an attending physician. Also, it is imperative that resident physicians assume significant responsibility in patient care before they become attending physicians. Every great attending physician was once a resident in need of experience that could only be gained by managing a patient's agenda directly. Having said that, I have no doubt that many would argue vociferously that it is immoral to have such distinctions in patient care. They would say the patients should be randomly assigned to caretakers — including residents — which would give resident physicians the necessary experience to one day assume the role of attending physician.

A few years ago, I was consulted by a woman who was thirty-three-weeks pregnant with a baby who had been diagnosed by ultrasound to have hydrocephalus or water on the brain. She was on her way to Kansas at the recommendation of her local obstetrician to have an abortion, as Kansas was the only state that would allow a baby to be aborted that was perfectly viable outside the womb without life support. I discussed with her in great detail the implications of having a baby with hydrocephalus, and I discussed with her the many options that were available. In the end, she decided to complete the pregnancy, and we were able to place a shunt in the baby after it was born to divert excess fluid away from the brain. Although the baby had some developmental delays, she continues to thrive today.

Some years ago, I was discussing this case with the head of the ACLU, who had made a statement that the purpose of their organization was to speak for and defend those who could not speak for and defend themselves. I asked whether or not this thirty-three-week-old fetus qualified as a human being incapable of speaking for or defending itself. He artfully dodged answering the question, so I decided to make it easier for him. I told him that there were many premature infants in our neonatal intensive care unit who were several weeks younger than the baby in question. These babies were on life support, but in most cases we had every expectation that they would survive. I asked him if he would speak for and defend the rights of a twenty-eight-week-old baby who was in an incubator and on life support. He replied that that was a no-brainer; of course the ACLU would defend such an individual. As you might imagine, I then asked why it was difficult to defend a baby that was five weeks further along in development and was in the most protected environment possible, but easy to defend a less viable individual who was outside of the womb. He realized his answers were not logical, he said, but he felt that ultimately a woman had the right to terminate a pregnancy until the second that the child is born. This situation perhaps crystallizes one of the major moral dilemmas we face in American society today: Does a woman have the right to terminate another human life because it is encased in her body? Does ownership convey absolute power of life and death over the owned subject? If it does, then NFL quarterback Michael Vick was unfairly imprisoned for torturing and killing dogs in Atlanta.

STILL PAYING FOR OUR SORDID MORAL PAST

During some of our darker periods of American history, when slavery was legal, slave owners felt they had the right to do anything they wanted to their slaves since they were their property. They believed with a passion that the abolitionists were interfering in matters that did not concern them, and they saw no reason why they could not sexually abuse their slaves, beat them, torture them—even kill them at will. But in spite of the concept of one human owning another being so fundamentally despicable and immoral, we were one of the last nations to abolish slavery.

It is not difficult to see why it took the United States so long to join other civilized nations of ridding ourselves of this atrocity. Slave labor was essential to the financial well-being of our fledgling nation, and without it, our struggle for recognition and economic power would probably have had a different outcome.

Since the Bible admonishes slaves to be obedient to their masters, slave owners felt that there was a biblical "stamp of approval" for their activities, which allowed them to live with their guilt. The fact that people willfully broke up families simply for economic gain shows how easily we humans can ignore and justify indescribable inhumanity to our fellow man when we stand to benefit personally. Of course, some slave owners treated their slaves with some degree of respect and even love. Such individuals were in turn respected and loved by their slaves. Such a relationship in no way justifies the institution of slavery, but simply points out a multiplicity of complex relationships.

Not all Americans were in favor of slavery; in fact, the opposition by some was so strong that it threatened to destroy the fragile union that existed between the original thirteen colonies. This sentiment was strongly voiced in the delegates' discourse in 1787, during the convention in Philadelphia called to revise the Articles of Confederation. Abolitionists led by the Quakers were relentless in their calls for doing away with slavery. After intense and rancorous debates, representatives from the smaller states and larger states finally agreed on a compromise: they would allow the slave states to join the union, but slaves would only be counted as three-fifths of a person for the purposes of establishing the appropriate number of representatives for each state. This was also supposed to be a temporary situation, and there was a general understanding in the union that slavery would soon be abolished because it was both immoral and inconsistent with the concept of a nation for, of, and by the people. Nevertheless, slavery continued for another three-quarters of a century, accompanied by untold atrocities, including vicious rapes and murders. Immorality was widespread, no matter how you looked at it.

I don't think many question whether slavery was immoral or not; obviously it was, but does that mean that we continue to tip the scales the other way forever because of mistakes that were made more than a century ago? Certain individuals feel that the United States cannot be forgiven for slavery until reparations are made to the descendants of slaves. This belief goes back to Mosaic laws requiring anyone who caused harm to someone else to make reparations to that individual or to the family if the injured individual was dead. There certainly is precedence for reparations in America. Many Native American tribes whose ancestors were deprived of land and resources were given sweetheart deals by our government, which now allows them to own some of the largest and most lucrative gambling casinos in the world.

Many years ago, I was asked to speak at an all-tribe graduation for a large group of Native Americans who owned a massive gambling casino complex. Elders of the tribe told me that they were hoping that I could inspire many of the unmotivated young people to attend college, which the tribe would happily pay for. Since the tribe had so much money, many of the teenagers were happy to drive around in their BMWs and party instead of taking advantage of educational opportunities that would ensure a positive future for the tribe. The reparations the tribe had received were certainly justified given the tremendous losses suffered by Native Americans at the hands of American settlers, but I'm not entirely certain that the end result benefited the tribe as it could have.

I can also understand the idea of reparations for the Japanese-American families who were unjustly interned during World War II. In that case, corrective action was taken at a time when many of the victims could actually benefit from it. In the case of slavery, however, there are neither slaves nor slave owners currently living, so it seems unfair to require people who had nothing to do with slavery to pay for it. I understand the argument that the descendants of slave owners inherited property and large sums of money accumulated through slave labor, and are thus obligated to share the proceeds with the descendants of slaves. There is some legitimacy to such an argument, but no one can really quantify the percentage of assets derived from slave labor in order to distribute them.

Furthermore, where do you draw the line for reparations in the past? If you kept going back you would soon be pre-dating the existence of the United States, Europe, Asia, and Africa. Obviously it is unfair to arbitrarily pick a date or event and say that reparations should commence from that point forward. As Proverbs 17:9 reminds us, peace is more likely when one forgets about past wrongs as opposed to reminding others of them. And if we all concentrate on building on the opportunities that exist and creating a more motivating environment to encourage individuals to achieve, the sky is the limit.

If slavery had ended and everyone had been treated as equals from that point on, it might be easier to excuse the immorality that permitted hundreds of years of slavery in America. Unfortunately, slavery was followed by a system of sharecropping that exploited labor by former slaves, so that effectively they were still slaves. Jim Crow laws also kept African-Americans in a position of servitude both economically and socially. Fatal beatings and lynchings were commonplace throughout the South even into the 1970s. So on the issue of morality with respect to treating one's fellow man fairly, I think we deserve a failing grade. That does not mean that things have not improved substantially over the last four decades, but four decades does not erase four centuries of brutal oppression.

Even today we exploit our fellow human beings for work. Is it moral for us, for example, to take advantage of cheap labor from illegal immigrants while denying them citizenship? I'm sure you can tell from the way I phrased the question that I believe we have taken the moral low road on this issue. Some segments of our economy would virtually collapse without these undocumented workers—we all know that—yet we continue to harass and deport many individuals who are simply seeking a better life for themselves and their families. Is there a way to apply logic to this issue and arrive at an intelligent solution?

All we have to do is look to our northern neighbor, Canada. They have a guest worker program,[1] which allows people to enter the country as officially recognized guest workers who pay taxes, receive benefits, and are able to come and go as they please without infringing on anyone else's rights. They have the reassuring knowledge that they have contributed to the local economy while at the same time helping their families at home. Why is immigration such a difficult issue for us to deal with? I believe we are so tempted to play politics with this issue that both logic and morality have been thrown out of the window.

WHAT IS A JUST WAR?

What does the fact that we are so often involved in conflicts with other nations say about our morality? Since the inception of our nation, there have been very few extensive periods of peace. To approach the question another way, does an individual of high moral standing frequently find himself fighting with others? By bringing it down to an individual level, it is easier to see that the number of conflicts does not predict the level of morality. Instead, we need to first look at the reasons for the various wars before commenting on their morality.

Most of our numerous conflicts could be justified based on our national interests, and even though there were always protesters to our wars, few conflicts were considered immoral until the Vietnam War came along. Many said that stopping communism's spread was a noble goal and fully justified our involvement in this war, but others argued with some validity that we had no right to assume that our way of governing was superior to communism. As a student at Yale, I can remember these boisterous protests against the war, which echoed on college campuses across the nation.

During that war in the jungles of Vietnam, we burned villages with napalm and destroyed the lives of many innocent villagers who had nothing to do with the political struggle. The Vietcong forces had the tremendous advantage of knowing both the terrain and the people, which eventually afforded them victory in the war. Even though we had overwhelming force, we had no way to deploy it in jungle terrain. Many of our soldiers were not clear about their overall mission, which surely had a negative effect on their enthusiasm. If communist forces had been trying to invade the United States, there would have been no question about the goals of the military and the country at large, and no sacrifice would have been too great in order to achieve victory. There also would have been no question about the morality of defending our way of life in our own country. Since the Vietnam conflict ended poorly, our nation experienced a period of shame and humiliation for which the military was blamed, and many of the returning veterans were treated with disrespect. The Vietnam War[2] dampened America's enthusiasm for war, and we experienced one of the longest periods of peace in our nation's history.

However, sixteen years after the Vietnam War ended, Saddam Hussein invaded Kuwait and the enthusiasm for military intervention was tremendous. After the successful conclusion of the effort to restore freedom to Kuwait, President George H. W. Bush and the military heroes enjoyed enormous popularity and approval. A war with well-defined and widely accepted goals that ends in victory will virtually always be seen as virtuous. The subsequent war with Iraq[3] years later was much more controversial, especially after weapons of mass destruction were not found. Although a qualified victory was eventually scored, the opposition to it certainly rivaled that present during the Vietnam War. Whether the war in Iraq was moral or not is highly debatable. If you think stopping a brutal dictator from continuing to kill hundreds of thousands of his own people is worthwhile, then you are more likely to believe that we acted in a morally justifiable manner. If you are more concerned about the over 4,000 American lives that were lost and the hundreds of billions of dollars that were added to our national debt to be passed along to our children, then you're more likely to feel that our efforts were immoral.

The point here is that it is very difficult to determine our nation's morality based on its military conflicts. Also, because we have dramatic changes of leadership and political philosophy, we do not have a consistent policy that governs military intervention. Then too one can legitimately ask the question, is any war moral? We try to sanitize wars by establishing all kinds of rules of conduct. Certainly women and children should be spared and torture should not be used, along with a myriad of other guidelines. If we followed this line of reasoning regarding prohibitions in war to its logical conclusion, I think the ultimate rule would say no war, period! If you can establish arbitrary rules for war, then making one more rule that eliminates all war makes a lot of sense. Of course, by definition, wars tend to start when logical, reasoned diplomacy fails.

FAMILY VALUES AND EDUCATION

It is hard to talk about the morality of a nation without considering the question of family values and the education of our youth. As we discussed in chapter 4, our founding fathers placed great importance on educating future generations. "I think with you," Benjamin Franklin once said, "that nothing is of more importance for the public weal [or welfare], than to form and train up youth in wisdom and virtue. Wise and good men are, in my opinion, the strength of the state; more so than riches or arms. I think also, that general virtue is more probably to be expected and obtained from the education of youth, than from the exhortations of adult persons; bad habits and vices of the mind being, like diseases of the body, more easily prevented than cured. I think, moreover, that the talents for the education of youth are the gift of God; and that he on whom they are bestowed, whenever a way is opened for the use of them, is as strongly called as if he heard a voice from heaven...."[4]

I believe one of the reasons our nation prospered was a strong emphasis on traditional family values that included instruction on the difference between right and wrong, teaching that began in the home and continued at school. And one of the central sources for defining values was the Bible, which back then was found in all public schools. Basic religious principles were taught in public schools in such a way as to have the broadest possible application without favoring any particular denomination. Children were taught that there was a Creator to whom they were responsible and that there was a moral code given to us by the Creator to whom we would all have to answer in the afterlife. The founding fathers had much to say regarding the morality of our nation and how important it was to our future, but I think one of the best quotes that summarizes their feelings is from John Adams when he said, "Our Constitution was made only for a moral and religious people. It is wholly inadequate to the government of any other."[5]

I fully recognize that many in our society would prefer not to derive their morality from the Bible and its teachings. Many such people are atheists or agnostics and claim to have their own internal moral compass. While their opinions diverge when it comes to sex outside of marriage, homosexuality, gambling, the use of illicit drugs and alcohol, and other social behavior, I find it interesting to note, however, that their moral compass points in very much the same direction as Judeo-Christian values when it comes to such issues as murder, lying, cheating, and theft.

There is no question that the perspective over the last few decades regarding social morality has changed dramatically. When I was a child, it was generally considered shameful to have a child out of wedlock, whereas today, in many segments of our society, having a child out of wedlock is the norm, not in any way assigned social stigma. Many people feel this indicates that we are progressing to a more enlightened stage and that we are less judgmental and more accepting of everyone. Although being open-minded and accepting is generally a good thing, we should examine the effect this change in attitude has on society as a whole.

Children born out of wedlock are at least twice as likely to live in poverty as those born to a traditional family consisting of a married father and mother with a stable household income.[6] Unwed mothers are also more likely to be high school or college dropouts and are more likely to be recipients of public welfare—frequently on a chronic basis. There is a greater incidence of sexually transmitted diseases in both unwed mothers and unwed fathers. Not only are these things deleterious to the affected children and parents, but they also place extra burdens on the rest of society, who has to pay the bills. And because someone else pays the bill, the behavior continues, and we feed an entitlement society with a voracious appetite for government funding.

This brings us back to our point that what appears to be good in the short run, but is harmful in the long run, is in the end not virtuous and does not contribute to societal morality. A truly moral nation enacts policies that encourage personal responsibility and discourage self-destructive behavior by not subsidizing people who live irresponsibly and make poor choices. This can be done in a compassionate way by phasing out government assistance for those already receiving it and by making it clear that there will be no government assistance in the future in these situations. This is not to say that the affected individuals cannot be aided by their families, churches, and other charitable organizations and individuals. What we have just discussed may seem a bit harsh to many bleeding heart do-gooders, but I submit that what is harsh is continuing to encourage irresponsible behavior and generating a permanent underclass. We also simply cannot afford welfare programs for able-bodied people who make unwise choices and expect other people to pay for it.

An example of how responsible government policies can change a society's behavior is found in Sweden, where they decided in the 1990s that their nation's incidence of drunk driving was too high.[7] They changed the legally tolerated blood-alcohol limit from 0.05 to 0.02 (in the United States, the average tolerated blood-alcohol level is 0.08—four times higher than that in Sweden) and enacted and enforced severe penalties for drunk driving, including mandatory jail time, astronomical fines, and confiscation of one's vehicle. As a result, there was a dramatic decline in alcohol-related traffic accidents and fatalities. The behavioral changes are so enculturated that hardly anyone even considers driving if they have consumed a single can of beer. This shows that people do respond to appropriate legislative changes and that there is still great potential for our nation to use government in a responsible and uplifting manner that will not break the bank and that will encourage the development of responsible citizens who will be contributors rather than dependents.

FISCAL RESPONSIBILITY: A HALLMARK OF A MORAL GOVERNMENT

In 2008, we saw the beginning of a gigantic financial crisis on Wall Street, with financial experts convincing both Republicans and Democrats that a financial tsunami would destroy the United States and the rest of the world if a gigantic government bailout did not occur immediately. So our government embarked upon a series of financial ventures to prop up companies and financial entities that were "too big to fail."

Whether it really worked or not is anybody's guess and can never be proven one way or another, but one thing that did become clear was that there were many people involved in the financial markets who made enormous sums of money by engaging in questionable financial practices, while shareholders and constituents made little or nothing—or even lost great sums of money. Some of the tricks employed by money managers had been outlawed through wise legislative reforms enacted after the stock market crash in 1929 and the ensuing decade of turmoil. Congress recognized way back then that unless financial markets were regulated, greed would raise its ugly head and wreak havoc whenever human beings are involved.

During the 1990s, however, Congress allowed significant deregulation of financial markets, perhaps expecting that human nature had changed. It took almost twenty years to prove that greed was still alive and well, and it almost destroyed our nation. The obvious question given our subject matter is, does a moral nation allow criminals who have defrauded the populace to get away without penalty?

I have no problem with people making large sums of money legitimately along with all the other people involved in whatever venture is generating the money. On the other hand, just because people control our markets' financial instruments, they should not be able to personally benefit by manipulating those instruments to their advantage. Many of these people suffer from the same type of entitlement mentality seen in poor people who are always looking for a government handout. These Wall Street moguls and corporate executives actually think that what they do is worth hundreds of millions of dollars a year, even though in many cases they are simply moving money around, producing nothing. The jury is still out on whether our government will conduct a serious investigation into what manipulation, if any, lay behind this crisis and whether justice will be served.

The Bible says that "the love of money is a root of all kinds of evil" (1 Timothy 6:10), and with this basic principle in mind one can easily see how a government that is in love with the people's money could engage in the evil act of "bleeding the people." A truly virtuous government would act fiscally responsible, constantly remind itself of its duties, and collect just enough money through taxes to take care of those duties. It would never overspend its budget unless there was an emergency, in which case it would make every effort to pay back the debt as soon as possible. The United States government was very fiscally responsible up until World War II, after which time paying back the national debt became less of a priority. That debt has continued to grow and now is almost equal to our gross domestic product (GDP)[8]—an entire year's worth of our nation's production simply going to pay off debt.

There are many politicians who say we have always lived with a large national debt[9] and that it is really just a number that doesn't mean anything, but the founders of our nation would be astonished—even outraged—to hear our leaders saying such things. Thomas Jefferson said, "We shall all consider ourselves unauthorized to saddle posterity with our debts, and morally bound to pay them ourselves; and consequently within what may be deemed the period of a generation, or the life of the majority."[10]

One of the greatest responsibilities of parents is that of looking out for the future of their children. This is not only a duty, it is a moral obligation. The same is true of a nation and its progeny. To saddle the next generation with unimaginable debt is not only callous, it is morally reprehensible. How can we even live with ourselves knowing that we are eroding the standard of living of the next generations with each dollar that we add to the national debt?

As of this writing, a vigorous debate has taken place regarding the budget for the remainder of the fiscal year. The Republicans, driven by the new members of the Tea Party, wanted to cut $61 billion from the budget, while the Democrats were willing to cut only about one-sixth of that amount. The president, not wanting to be accused of cutting entitlements, took a "wait and see" attitude rather than leading the charge toward fiscal responsibility. Subsequently, after a huge tug-of-war between the White House, the Republicans, and the Democrats, a new bipartisan super committee has been established to make over a trillion dollars in budgeting cuts and stem the rise of our national debt. Perhaps they will be taken more seriously than was the Bowles/Simpson Commission on Fiscal Responsibility and Reform. Both Democrats and Republicans have strayed so far from the path of responsible financial policy that the concept of balancing the budget is foreign to them. I believe many of them simply cannot grasp the concept of only spending what you have. I do understand that making budgetary cuts will be painful, but it will not be nearly as painful as going bankrupt! One need only look at historic images of Hungarian pengo bills being swept in the gutter in 1946 or of the Zimbabwe one hundred trillion dollar bill created recently because of their rocketing hyperinflation[11] to understand the gravity of this situation.

Knowing how Washington works, I can already predict that our Democratic president and the rest of the Democratic Party will claim that the Republicans want to cut programs that benefit children, the elderly, and the infirm and that they want to stifle medical research and programs that will create economic growth. The Republicans will claim that the Democrats are addicted to spending and couldn't stop if their lives depended on it. Applying logic to the situation, which may be too much to hope for given all the emotions flying around Washington, could go a long way toward resolving the problem without making it into a political football.

I believe the logical approach would be to have each governmental agency and department trim its budget by 10 percent—with no exceptions. In each subsequent year, another 10 percent decrease would be required and would continue as long as necessary to bring the budget back into balance. This would mean there would be no sacred cows and no sparing of entitlements. No politician, agency, or special interest group could cry foul. Government agencies would either have to become much more efficient, cut benefits, or both, and those in charge of each governmental department should have the best idea of where the excess fat is and how to cut it in the least painful manner. Since the axe would fall equally on everyone, no one could claim that they were being unfairly targeted, and we could eliminate the political overtones and get down to business.

It is often easier to understand the insight logic brings to a situation by choosing a smaller and simpler problem to solve. If a family of seven—consisting of a father, mother, and five children—experienced a substantial financial setback, many lifestyle changes would have to take place. One of the changes might be the weekly allowance. I think all of the children would understand if their parents announced that due to budgetary constraints, instead of getting ten dollars a week, they would only receive nine dollars a week—and that if things did not change, further reductions of allowance might occur in the future. Although none of the children would be happy about this change, they would be satisfied that everyone had shared equally in the sacrifice. On the other hand, if the parents decided that two of the children really were too important to have to suffer a reduction in allowance, the other three siblings would protest that they were being treated unfairly, and fights might break out.

There are a whole host of other issues we could discuss and problems we could solve by applying logic and fairness—and discuss and solve them we must, for our solutions to today's problems have significant ramifications for tomorrow. Our problems are not ours alone—we share them with future generations—and we have a moral obligation to hand our nation over to our children and grandchildren in good shape.

If this task sounds impossible, I assure you that we can easily accomplish it if we are willing to embrace our United States Constitution and the principles put forth by the founders, who took their bearings from the Word of God. Short-term politically expedient "fixes" and morality are frequently incompatible, and moral values will only become a part of all our policies when we are willing to rediscover and embrace the principles that established our Constitution.

Morality, of course, must be based on something, and we in America have the luxury of freely deciding what that is. Although our founders felt quite comfortable with the Bible as their guidepost, we must now decide what constitutes the foundation of our morality today. Without a moral basis for the way we conduct ourselves, our values will continue to deteriorate, and with them our country's prosperity. We have made mistakes; however, there is always time to learn from them, change our direction, and move toward a better way.

CHAPTER 8

LEARNING FROM OUR MISTAKES

EVERY PERSON MAKES MISTAKES, so it should come as no surprise that every nation of the world has made mistakes as well. Talk with a German national about the hope their country placed in Hitler's rise to power on the heels of the Great Depression. Or consider our own nation's internment of Japanese-Americans during World War II, and you'll agree that the question is not *whether* a nation makes mistakes; the question is whether a nation learns from its mistakes, builds on that knowledge it gains over time, and grows in wisdom. Those nations who learn from their mistakes will become wise, while those who repeat the same mistakes over and over again, expecting a different result, are foolish.

I certainly experienced my share of mistakes growing up. Because of the racial and socioeconomic injustice I experienced as a boy, in my anger and frustration I began to retaliate by going after people with baseball bats, rocks, and knives. One day a boy pushed me too far. I told him to back off, but he wouldn't quit pestering me. Finally, I pulled out my knife and lunged at him, striking him in the abdomen. He fell back, and for a moment I thought I had killed him, but just then my knife blade fell to the ground. It had hit his belt buckle and snapped in two.

I ran into the bathroom and locked myself in, terrified that I had just tried to kill someone—and over something so trivial. If his belt buckle had not been there, I would have seriously injured or killed him, and I would have been on my way to reform school or jail, following the path of so many around me.

All of my life I had attended church services, and I knew—at least in theory—that God could radically change a person's life for the better. I also knew that I had tried to gain control of my temper time after time with repeated failure. Although I was only fourteen years old, I was familiar with behavioral modification therapy from reading *Psychology Today*—but I was also acutely aware that we had no money for behavioral modification therapy. By that time I was a straight-*A* student, yet I recognized that I would never achieve my dreams of becoming a physician as long as I harbored an uncontrollable temper.

So I fell to my knees there on the bathroom floor, pleading with God to remove my temper. There was a Bible in the bathroom, and I opened it to the book of Proverbs. Verses about anger and the folly of a fool's actions all seemed written to me and about me. Other verses encouraged me, such as Proverbs 16:32, which says that mightier is the man who can control his temper than the man who can conquer a city. I stayed in that bathroom for three hours, reading, contemplating, and praying. My selfishness had made me so angry inside, and it dawned on me that if I could just step outside myself and look at things from someone else's point of view, I might see the world differently and not feel so persecuted.

My new, God-given perspective worked like a charm. He became very real to me that day, and I have never had another angry outburst of uncontrollable temper since then. There would be other tests, of course, and I would make my share of mistakes. But that, after all, is how we learn and grow.

My high school, Southwestern High School in Detroit, was not particularly well known for its academics, but it was a football and basketball powerhouse. It won several state basketball championships, and you reached the pinnacle of respect among your peers if you were a starter on one of the varsity sports teams. The only other way to gain recognition was to join a successful singing group. Since we were located in Motown,[1] students always expected one of the groups to make it big.

I was definitely not one of the cool guys, however. They always wore the latest fashions, knew the latest "jams" on the radio, sported a nice car, and had three "chicks" on each arm. They also had a distinctive walk known as "the Detroit strut" and an ever-changing lingo that denoted how "hip" they were.

I, on the other hand, was a total nerd, complete with stacks of books, thick glasses, a slide rule, and clean but dated clothing. I had neither a car nor a girlfriend. Nevertheless, I was certain I would make my mark in the world, because I was going to be so smart that everyone was going to have to take notice of me. But all I really got during my freshman year was ridicule, and I began to feel very out of place. By the time my sophomore year rolled around, I was ready to abandon my nerdy appearance and become one of the cool guys. I began to play basketball late into the night, and more disturbingly, I began grumbling constantly to my mother about my "uncool" clothing. My mother was very disappointed that I had lost my way and was heading in the same direction as all the people she characterized as losers. Despite her arguments, I complained incessantly.

One day, during one of our arguments, she thrust at me all the money she had made scrubbing floors and cleaning toilets and said in frustration, "You pay the bills, you buy the food, you pay the rent and take care of all the other necessities. With *all* the money you have left over, feel free to buy all the cool clothes you want."

I was thrilled, because I figured I was finally going to have my way and become one of the cool guys. As I started allocating money for all the expenses, however, I quickly ran out. I soon realized that my mother was a financial genius to somehow keep us fed and sheltered. I felt like a total fool and sheepishly returned the money to her. I never complained about my clothing again.

Fortunately, having read the Bible over the preceding years, I quickly recognized that my desire to be part of the "in crowd" was more characteristic of a fool than a person of accomplishment. During my slide into foolishness, my grades had slipped precipitously, and I was horrified as I looked in the mirror and realized what I was becoming. I immediately corrected my course, abandoning any desire to be one of the cool guys. I once again became a diligent student, and my grades dramatically improved. From that day forward I was never again tempted to abandon my long-term goals for the sake of momentary acceptance.

The excitement I had experienced as a freshman in high school was nothing compared to the exhilaration I felt at becoming a "Yale man." Going from inner-city Detroit to the ivy-covered walls of Yale was certainly a culture shock; rich wood paneling covered the dining hall walls, the plates were real china, and the eating utensils were real silver. Works of art adorned the walls, and Oriental rugs covered the hardwood floors. I had gone from dire poverty to the lap of luxury overnight—and I intended to enjoy every minute of it.

Obtaining top grades in high school had been a snap. The material was so easy I could study for half an hour before an exam and still get an *A*. I naturally assumed I could do the same thing at Yale, so I took judo classes, played ping-pong and table soccer, watched television, attended live entertainment events, and generally had fun. I thought I had corrected my academic flaws in high school, but academic success in a high-powered university obviously required significantly more correction than I had accomplished. By midterm, I began to worry a bit because I wasn't doing well in some classes, including freshman chemistry, which was a prerequisite for those planning to go to medical school. My concern wasn't enough to stop me from having fun, but it did dampen my enthusiasm.

By the time final exams rolled around, however, my grade in chemistry was so low I would have failed the course even if I had gotten an *A* on the final exam. In an act of great compassion (or sadism, I'm not sure which), the chemistry professor offered to give anyone who was failing the course double credit for the final exam—which gave me one last glimmer of hope. I suspect he believed that people like me had no chance of passing the final exam if they had done so poorly throughout the course of the semester; therefore, there was little or no risk in making such an offer.

The night before the final exam I sat in my room with my thick chemistry textbook, a barrier to all my hopes and dreams. I poured out my heart to God, asking forgiveness for squandering such a wonderful educational opportunity. I asked him to show me what he really wanted me to do with my life, since I obviously wasn't going to get into medical school. Preferably, I asked him to work a miracle. As I tried futilely to memorize my entire chemistry textbook, I fell asleep and entered a dream.

During that dream I was the only student in a large auditorium, and a nebulous figure was writing out chemistry problems on the chalkboard. I awakened early that morning with the dream so vivid in my mind that I quickly consulted my chemistry textbook to corroborate what I had seen in the dream. When I opened the test booklet the next day during the chemistry final exam, I was flabbergasted when I recognized each of the problems in the booklet as one of the problems that the nebulous figure was working out on the chalkboard in my dream. It felt like I was in the twilight zone as I hurriedly scribbled down the answers, afraid that I would forget them if I waited too long.

I knew the moment I finished the exam that God had granted me my miracle. I promised God that he would never have to do such a thing for me again and that I would become a diligent student and make him proud of me. It was a scary lesson to learn, but it profoundly changed my attitude about my purpose in college.

The rest of my time at Yale was relatively smooth sailing, but medical school was another matter. The amount of new material that must be mastered in medical school is equivalent to learning several foreign languages simultaneously, and many students flunked out before the first year was over. I had learned my lesson in college and was very diligent about studying and attending all my lectures, but I still did horribly on the first set of comprehensive examinations. As a result, I was required to see my counselor who had been assigned by the university to help me get through medical school. He told me that I should simply drop out of medical school since I obviously wasn't cut out for medicine. Of course I was crushed, because the only career I had aspired to since I was eight years old was that of a physician.

Following that meeting, I returned to my apartment and again poured out my heart to God, begging for wisdom. As I prayed, a thought occurred to me. *What kind of courses have you always struggled with,* I asked myself, *and what kind of courses have given you no difficulty?* It dawned on me that I did very well in courses that required a lot of reading, and I struggled in courses in which the material was communicated through boring lectures. Unfortunately, I was being subjected to six to eight hours of boring lectures every day in medical school. Right there and then, I made an executive decision to skip the boring lectures and to spend that time reading. It was a risky move, but if it didn't yield results, I would have been in no worse shape than I was in already. It turned out to be a fabulously successful strategy, and the rest of medical school was a snap.

That traumatic episode taught me how important it was to learn your own strengths and weaknesses from your mistakes. Over the subsequent years, I have saved enormous time and effort by understanding that I gain nothing from listening to boring lectures. I did learn that I respond well to visual input, such as reading books, viewing images, and using flashcards. I'm convinced that much of the success I have experienced in life is a result of learning from my failures.

LESSONS FROM OUR MISTAKE OF ALLOWING SLAVERY

Of all the mistakes our nation has engaged in, allowing the practice of slavery was obviously one of our most egregious. I have found that when I extol the virtues of our nation, particularly on college campuses, the question of slavery frequently comes up—and this, of course, casts a huge shadow on many of the outstanding accomplishments of our leaders over the course of our nation's history. I doubt that there are many people today who would try to justify slavery, and it's safe to say there is general agreement that it was an abomination. But what did we learn from this mistake?

I hope we learned that all men are indeed created equal, and that given proper opportunities, not only can they improve their personal lot in life, but through the development of their intellect they can make substantial contributions to society at large. In the case of African-Americans, all you have to do is open your eyes to see the many contributions they have made to the welfare of our nation.

When you see a light, for instance, you may think of Thomas Edison, but it was his right-hand man, Louis Latimer, an African-American, who developed the filament for the lightbulb, allowing it to function for more than two or three days. He also invented the electric lamp, did pioneering work in incandescent lighting, and diagrammed the telephone for Alexander Graham Bell, among other things. The traffic signal was invented by Garrett Morgan, an African-American who also invented the gas mask, which saved many lives during wars. From the potato chip to the ironing board, from refrigeration systems to sound equipment such as the microphone chip, many items that we use on a regular basis were invented by African-American individuals,[2] who were once relegated simply to the role of slave.

If we as a nation learn the inherent value of every citizen, our policies will strive to cultivate that talent to benefit us all. The fact that we have not recognized a high school dropout rate of 30 percent as a national disaster shows that we have yet to fully comprehend the value of each individual. Not only are we failing to reap substantial benefits from these individuals, but in many cases we are actually depleting our coffers by paying for them in the penal system or the welfare system. Any one of these young people with proper encouragement and education could potentially come up with innovative products or helpful services. But because of our history of segregation, Jim Crowism, and racism, generations of African-Americans have grown up with a sense of alienation toward their own country. This has created extreme levels of cynicism and distrust among many citizens who might otherwise have been enthusiastic supporters of the nation.

I have heard it said that everybody harbors some degree of racism, but my own observations have led me to believe that individuals who are well-educated and who think deeply about matters tend to not base any biases on superficial characteristics. Such people tend to realize that it is the brain that makes the person who they are, not the external covering. People who are less intellectually sophisticated tend to allow their emotions to be affected by very superficial things, such as skin color. Unfortunately, basing one's ideas and opinions on superficial traits is rather common in places where intellectual development is not highly rewarded or praised. I suspect that if one did an in-depth study of people who arbitrarily engage in racial bias, they would find that such people were also attracted to visually appealing but unhealthy foods. They might be more inclined to go for the flashy red car than the dull gray hybrid that gets fifty miles to a gallon of gasoline. These people come in all sizes, colors, shapes, and socioeconomic categories, and rather than shun and castigate such people, our nation's goal should be to educate them and fill in the intellectual gaps, which would improve their value both to themselves and to us all.

As an intern at Johns Hopkins in 1977, I was frequently mistaken for an orderly, phlebotomist, respiratory therapist, or some position other than a doctor. For most, it was an innocent mistake; however, it would have been easy for them to notice that I had a stethoscope around my neck. Or that I was in scrubs, or was wearing a white lab coat, which would have been extremely unusual for an orderly. When I would gently point out that I was a doctor, the majority of people were highly embarrassed and apologetic. I tried to alleviate their discomfort by letting them know that I was in no way offended and that I could easily have made a similar mistake. I never encountered anyone who made that same mistake twice. I helped eliminate their social ignorance, which I'm sure was beneficial to them in the long run.

STILL SHAKING SHALLOW, RACIST THINKING

Although much overt racism has been eliminated in America, there are still too many people who make sweeping generalizations about whole groups of people based on a negative encounter with a person of a different race. In order to resolve this problem, we must first admit that it exists even in our own families or ourselves — and African-Americans are just as likely to harbor racist attitudes as white people.

Just prior to the last presidential election, when the first African-American was elected president of the United States, I saw on television a segment where a reporter was interviewing African-Americans in Harlem, New York, about various policies advocated by candidate Barack Obama. All of the interviewees enthusiastically supported each policy discussed without knowing that they were actually the policies held by candidate John McCain. The most hilarious part of the interviews occurred when the people were asked what they thought about Senator Obama's choice of his running mate, Sarah Palin. The answers were all quite favorable toward Governor Palin because she was picked, they thought, by Obama. Many African-Americans voted for Obama simply because he was a black man and not because they resonated philosophically with his policies. If the situation were reversed, and white people were obviously voting for their candidate based on race and not political philosophy, shouts of racism would be deafening.

I do, however, understand the enormous pride African-Americans have because the president of the United States is a black man. I even know staunchly conservative African-Americans who voted for Obama even though they vehemently opposed his political platform. One individual told me that it wasn't really racism, but rather just a matter of being overwhelmed by emotion upon entering the voting booth. But racism is a subset of hatred, which also is an emotion. I'm sure many white voters were overwhelmed by emotion several years ago during California's 1982 race for governor, when they couldn't bring themselves to vote for Tom Bradley, who was the mayor of Los Angeles at the time and happened to be an African-American. All the pre-election polls showed Bradley far ahead of his white opponent, and it was a foregone conclusion that he was going to win and become California's first African-American governor—but when it came time to cast votes, sentiment swung radically in the other direction. Voting for Barack Obama simply because he is black is just as irrational and racist as not voting for Tom Bradley because he was black.

As a nation, we must first admit that we have a problem with racism and shallow thinking, and we need to redouble our efforts to learn from the ugly episodes in our history and move forward—united—to tackle real problems.

COMPOUNDING OUR MISTAKES FINANCIALLY

Because President Obama is an African-American who believes in redistributing wealth, white people might wonder if all or most black people are like President Obama and want to redistribute wealth. However, I personally know many African-Americans who vigorously disagree with the concept of government redistribution of wealth. They love this country and have put forth a great deal of physical and intellectual effort to succeed in our nation. They share the same values as the majority of Americans and believe that they should be able to keep or distribute their resources as they see fit.

When the government becomes large and intrusive and feels that it has the right to as much of the resources owned by the people as it wants, then we have clearly strayed away from some of the foundational principles of this nation. What is truly amazing is how accepting most Americans are of this government intrusion into our lives and bank accounts. It is commonplace today to find large groups of people who believe the government has a responsibility to take care of all the basic necessities of its citizens. Benjamin Franklin, however, wrote:

> To relieve the misfortunes of our fellow creatures is concurring with the Deity; it is godlike; but, if we provide encouragement for laziness, and supports for folly, may we not be found fighting against the order of God and nature, which perhaps has appointed want and misery as the proper punishments for, and cautions against, as well as necessary consequences of, idleness and extravagance? Whenever we attempt to amend the scheme of Providence, and to interfere with the government of the world, we had need be very circumspect, lest we do more harm than good.[3]

In this passage and in many of his other writings, Franklin makes it clear that kindness and charity are admirable traits, but that it is actually destructive to continually support the needs and habits of those who are lazy and irresponsible. By doing so, we only encourage the proliferation of these undesirable traits and the numbers of people who have to be supported. Samuel Adams went right to the heart of the matter when he said, "The utopian schemes of leveling (redistribution), and a community of goods (the government owns everything), are as visionary and impractical as those which vest all property in the Crown."[4] These ideas he even called unconstitutional.

I believe we are in the process right now of learning that our government is far too big — and the bigger it gets, the more taxpayer money it needs to sustain itself. A gigantic, bloated government has to keep itself busy in order to justify its existence; hence, you have more regulations and meddling in the affairs of the people, whether they request it, need it, or not. Our government is now so large and expensive that each year our national debt grows larger. Currently it sits between $14 and $15 trillion — a number that is so large that it is virtually incomprehensible. That comes out to $50,000 for every man, woman, and child in the United States.

It was obviously a mistake to allow our government to reach this size and to spend as much as it has, but it is not the fault of one party or the other. Rather, it is the natural tendency of government to expand if there is no conscientious effort to keep it under control. The Constitution of the United States was written in such a way as to restrain government growth and power if there was the will to adhere to it, but unfortunately many of our legislators feel that the Constitution is outdated and largely irrelevant to today's society. They feel that we have advanced far beyond the understanding of the founding fathers and that through appropriate government, we can create a better life for everyone. They may be right, but I doubt it. The reason I'm skeptical that we need a new government is that the old government worked so well. Our early, limited government provided an atmosphere that encouraged productivity and innovation, resulting in the most rapid expansion of a powerful middle class that the world had ever seen. It resulted in enormous economic and industrial power as well as an extremely educated populace. If you have something that works, why change it?

Is there a logical solution for controlling the size of our government and the resulting size of our national deficit? Currently the debate is raging in Washington between the Republicans, who have been largely co-opted by the Tea Party, and the Democrats, who are finding it very difficult to break out of their tax-and-spend mode. The Democrats accuse Republicans of draconian budget cuts that would take food out of the mouths of babies and shelter from the elderly. At the same time, the Republicans accuse the Democrats of having no concern for our future generations and no understanding of the concept of budgetary constraints. Who is right and who is wrong in this exaggerated tug-of-war is not nearly as important as how to solve the problem. The problem is our mistake of permitting a bloated government bureaucracy that requires unimaginable amounts of money to sustain itself. And our problem is magnified by numerous special interest groups advocating to protect their pet programs from a reduction in government spending.

As a nation, we have become so accustomed to ever-rising taxes that the fact that the government takes up to half of all one's income does not really faze many people anymore. Our government would do well to remember that one of the major reasons for the Revolutionary War was excessive taxation. I will admit to making a very good living, and I am grateful to live in this country and to have been afforded the opportunity to obtain a first-rate education and pursue the career of my choosing. However, my biggest expense by far is taxes. Between federal, state, local, sales, and real estate taxes, more than half of my income goes to pay taxes. Since that is the case, you might say that I work for the government. This is certainly not the kind of situation that was envisioned by the founding fathers.

THE FOUNDING FATHERS ON FINANCIAL RESPONSIBILITY

It is clear from the writings of our founding fathers that they disagreed with such excessive taxation to redistribute wealth. In the Annals of Congress (House of Representatives, 3rd Congress, 1794), President James Madison is documented as saying, "I cannot undertake to lay my finger on that article of the Constitution which granted a right to Congress of expending, on objects of benevolence, the money of their constituents."

We all want to be benevolent, of course, but as President Madison pointed out, there is nothing in the Constitution that entitles the government to use the money of their constituents for charitable purposes, no matter how noble their goals. His quote should be read every day to members of our current Congress, particularly to those who complain about restraining the sacred entitlements to which our population has become addicted. Again our goals should be to reinstill a sense of independence and self-reliance in all of our citizens while continuing to cultivate caring and compassion for our neighbors who cannot take care of themselves.

Thomas Jefferson, an incredible visionary, made it clear that the accumulation of huge debt by the government is not only unacceptable, but dangerous to the preservation of our nation. "I place economy among the first and most important virtues," he said, "and public debt as the greatest of dangers. To preserve our independence, we must not let our rulers load us with perpetual debt."[5] It almost seems as if he had the ability to look into the future and recognize the natural consequences of ever-growing and unrestrained government. "The principle of spending money to be paid by future generations," he added, "under the name of funding, is but swindling futurity on a large scale."[6] Many voices today decry the accumulation of debt we're passing on to the next generation, but their protests are falling on many deaf ears among our leaders in government. But it is this statement of his that is especially alarming given the stated goals of the current administration to redistribute wealth: "The democracy will cease to exist when you take away from those who are willing to work and give to those who would not."[7] I hope this quote shakes you to the core, as it does me, and that you will realize how far we have strayed from the ideas of those who founded our nation and set it on a course of unparalleled success.

Jefferson was not alone in his views, and even some of his political foes embraced the ideas that are paramount to protecting our liberties and the prosperity of our nation. James Madison said, "If Congress can employ money indefinitely to the general welfare.... the powers of Congress would subvert the very foundation, the very nature of the limited government established by the people of America."[8] John Adams even appealed the matter to higher spiritual realities when he said, "The moment the idea is admitted into society that property is not as sacred as the laws of God, and that there is not a force of law and public justice to protect it, anarchy and tyranny commence."[9]

Would applying logic help in solving this problem of taxation? Certainly there have been many different schemes devised by mankind throughout history to impose and collect taxes. There is, however, only one tax imposed by God and that is the tithe, which is one-tenth of your salary. Interestingly, God did not say if you have a bumper crop that you should give triple tithes, nor did he say if your crops fail, you are entitled to a reduction in tithes or need to pay no tithes at all. This means that there is fairness in proportionality; if you make $10 billion a year, your tax or tithe would be $1 billion, whereas if your income is $10 a year, you would pay $1. Some would say that the billionaire is not hurt by his $1 billion contribution as much as the poor man who had to give up a dollar. They would say that the pain is not proportional and that the government has the right to decide how much more the rich man should pay. But where in God's law does it say that the rich man needs to give until it hurts? He just put $1 billion into the common pot, so why do we need to hurt him? It is this kind of thinking that has led to the proliferation of offshore bank accounts. If we had a proportional tax system, there would be no significant incentive for people to hide their money and they could spend more time concentrating on production, which in the long run would lead to even more money for the government. What about creating an atmosphere that encourages businesses to not hide their money, but to invest it back into the company to expand it and provide more jobs?

Our corporate tax rate is the second highest in the world. The only country with a higher corporate tax rate is Japan, which just so happens to also be the only country with a greater national debt than we have. Is that coincidence or evidence of cause and effect? I suspect the latter. By being shortsighted and greedy, our government is driving businesses to other countries, which deprives our people not only of jobs, but our government of vital income. If a low proportional tax rate is applied to everyone, including corporate entities, the flow of jobs and income would be into our nation rather than out of our nation. This is not complex economic theory, but rather common sense.

SIMPLIFY, SIMPLIFY, SIMPLIFY

In my many years as an academic physician, I have had the opportunity to hear many lectures by intellectuals from all over the world. Invariably, the best talks are not the ones that use complex terms and theories to demonstrate how brilliant the presenter is. Rather, the very best, most profound lectures are the ones that can easily be understood — even by those who are not experts in the field. I find that one has to have a very deep understanding of their subject matter in order to be able to break it down into commonsense language that anyone can comprehend and appreciate. The same is true of economists and politicians. Those with logical plans and straightforward common sense are easily understood. Meanwhile those who have no idea what they're talking about frequently make things far more complex than they need to be, and tell the people that they would understand it if only they were more knowledgeable and sophisticated.

Our founders knew that a slick politician can easily pull the wool over the eyes of an ignorant population, so they emphasized the importance of a broad, general education among the populace in order to maintain our freedom. I also believe, however, that legitimate political leaders have an obligation to explain their positions in a way that the common people can easily understand. As a neurosurgeon, I too have an obligation to explain the rationale for a complex operation that I propose in a way that allows the patient to make an intelligent decision. Any surgeon who cannot do that should not be operating, and the same is true of those running for political office.

Undoubtedly some critics will try to discredit me by saying, "He is a brilliant surgeon, but he knows nothing about politics, law, and economics, and should confine his opinions to medicine." As I already mentioned, however, five physicians signed the Declaration of Independence and several were signatories for the Constitution of the United States of America. In addition, physicians are the most highly educated group in the nation, trained to make decisions based on facts rather than emotion. They tend to be excellent with numbers, very concerned about the welfare of others, and accustomed to hard work. I speak at many medical school commencements and always encourage physicians to get involved in community affairs and in politics. In fact, I would love to see scientists and engineers get much more involved in the political process, bringing their no-nonsense common sense and logic to the table.

I am certainly not saying that people who are not physicians and scientists lack logical thinking skills—and it's sad that I even have to make such a disclaimer, but in our social milieu today, people who do not have very good arguments themselves tend to dissect every word of someone with whom they disagree in an attempt to make themselves look smart while discrediting someone else. Such tactics can be quite effective on people who do not think for themselves. This is another reason why our founding fathers placed so much emphasis on education for the common people—particularly on establishing values and understanding civics. They envisioned a government that was constantly changing its members, because by avoiding entrench-ment you disempower special interest groups and ensure fresh ideas. Since working for the government as a senator, representative, or staff person back then was not lucrative and required personal sacrifice, they never suspected that the system of government they put in place would be distorted by career politicians.

WHAT VALUES WILL HELP GUIDE US AWAY FROM FUTURE MISTAKES?

When our nation was rising rapidly to the pinnacle of the world, we were not ashamed of our relationship with God. In fact, reading from the Bible was not only common, it was expected in early public schools. The found-ers wanted generally accepted religious values to be taught in our schools without favoring any particular denomination, but they never intended to exclude God from the classroom,[10] because they knew that you had to have something upon which to base your system of values. If we only believe in evolution and survival of the fittest, whose values do we use to govern society?

Our society has become so paranoid about being politically incorrect that many people are afraid to say "Merry Christmas" simply because it contains the word *Christ*. Rather than spending so much time trying to figure out how not to offend people, it would be wonderful if we expended energy on teaching people not to be offended when someone offers a dif-ferent opinion. Our emphasis should not be on unanimity of speech and thought, but rather on learning to be respectful and courteous to those with different opinions. I am fond of saying that if two people think and say the same thing about everything, then one of them is not necessary. Also, if people can't hold honest conversations and are afraid to express their true feelings, conversations will necessarily be artificial, and it will be very dif-ficult to have a meaningful discourse and solve problems.

It is my hope and prayer that we will vigorously protect the rights of individuals and communities to live and believe as they please, as long as they do not infringe upon the rights of others. I hope we continue to protect the rights of our citizens to life, liberty, and the pursuit of happiness, not micromanaging their lives and imposing societal standards of political cor-rectness that impinge upon their liberty. These principles have nothing to do with liberalism or conservatism, but rather are the foundation that paved the way for the creation of the most successful and productive society the world has ever seen. We have had the opportunity to witness what works, and we have seen historically many examples of political systems that do not work.[11] Hopefully we will be wise enough to step back, take a deep breath, and critically analyze the triumphs and mistakes of our nation, and to use what we have learned to take another gigantic leap forward with liberty and justice for all.

CHAPTER 9

AMERICA'S ROLE IN A WORLD AT WAR

WHEN I WAS AN UNDERGRADUATE STUDENT AT YALE, the Vietnam War was still raging. Many students, frustrated by our nation's involvement in that war, referred to members of the military — including the National Guard — as "pigs," and anything having to do with our national defense as part of the "military-industrial complex." Even local police were generally regarded as part of the oppressive "establishment." This antigovernment attitude was so pervasive on the Yale campus that ROTC cadets were not required to wear their uniforms because officials feared they might be physically attacked.

The Vietnam War was, in retrospect, not a noble conflict. It brought shame to our nation because of both the outcome and the cause, and many people continue to bash the military and want to ban ROTC (Reserve Officers' Training Corps) from their college campuses. They believe the military is immoral and intellectually inferior. If they were a little more open-minded, however, they might realize that it takes tremendous intelligence and leadership to effectively command and control the massive global military infrastructure responsible for their freedom. Fortunately, we as a society have matured some since then, and even many of the far-left progressives commend the men and women of the military while condemning its actions. I speak at many college graduations and am proud to see the standing ovation that almost invariably occurs when graduates of the ROTC are recognized, something that never would have occurred three or four decades ago.

Except during the summer months, I am on a college campus almost on a weekly basis, and I greatly enjoy interacting with the bright young people who represent our future. Recently, I was thrilled to be invited to give a special lecture at the US Naval Academy in Annapolis, Maryland. The facility was immaculate and the cadets' demeanor was one of dignity, respect, and confidence. After interacting with several of them, I was very impressed with their knowledge and ability to express themselves. I subsequently discovered how rigorous the admissions process is, and I began to understand why so many of our military leaders are historically so intellectually accomplished. Seeing that sea of dress white uniforms was awe-inspiring, and the cadets were extremely attentive and receptive as I spoke. The pageantry I have witnessed over the years at Army, Navy, and Marine reviews is no façade, but reflects the pride and competence that characterizes our military.

My fascination with the military and its relationship to governing powers, along with my desire to wear the uniform, played a major role in my joining the ROTC back in high school. My brother, Curtis, who was a couple of years ahead of me, was a captain and company commander of our school unit when I joined, and his many ribbons and medals gave him universal respect both inside and outside of the ROTC world. I already had a great love for reading before involving myself in ROTC, so I was absolutely thrilled with all the books and manuals available to cadets — books on military strategy, martial law, explosives, map reading, and a myriad of other topics. I quickly rose through the ranks because of my acquisition of knowledge and observance of military protocol and dedication.

Because Baltimore is located so close to Washington, DC, the Pentagon, several military bases, and the Department of Defense, my wife and I have had the opportunity to befriend many military families. I love to play pool (billiards) and consider myself a pretty good player, but one day we were playing in the basement of my home when General Krulak, Commandant of the Marine Corps from the mid- to late 1990s, arrived. "What is that game you guys are playing?" he asked innocently. He then proceeded to clear the table without missing a single shot. He is an extremely bright, tactical, compassionate, and practical individual. He served in various commanding positions from Counter Guerilla Warfare School in Okinawa to Combat Development Command in Quantico, and after retiring from the Marine Corps, he successfully led the European division of MBNA, the nation's largest credit card company. He and his wife, Zandy, are great supporters of our Carson Scholars Fund and are wonderful role models for our young people. With leadership of his caliber, I am greatly comforted knowing our country is in great hands.

I first met General Colin Powell at a national conference in Detroit for which we were both keynote speakers. At that time, he was Chairman of the

Joint Chiefs and was already quite well known throughout the world. He was alert in noticing every detail about his environment and the people around him at every moment. His dignified but relaxed demeanor, and ability to speak competently to anyone on a wide range of subjects, inspired awe in everyone around him. I subsequently became a board member of his "America's Promise" organization and became even more impressed with his organizational skills and vision for our nation. Many of our former presidents, including George Washington, made their initial contributions to our society through their military participation, and I believe Colin Powell could probably have become the first African-American president of the United States.

Another admirable leader I've had the privilege to get to know, General Clara Adams-Ender, is a nurse who became the first African-American female to command a major Army base.[1] She may be short in stature, but she was a giant presiding over ceremonies at Fort Belvoir just outside of Washington, DC, a premier installation whose duties include entertaining visiting international dignitaries, such as Israeli military leader Moshe Dayan. It was thrilling to see this young woman review the troops, especially when her second-in-command was a young man appearing to be twice her height! When she retired from the military, she and her husband went on to establish their own successful business, and she continues to make her presence known. General Adams-Ender is yet another example of excellence at the helm of our military establishment.

One experience I lived through captures the clash in America regarding attitudes toward our military. In 1967, during my high school years in ROTC, the Detroit riots erupted, which were among the worst our nation has ever seen. Tanks rumbled down the street and squadrons of heavily armed soldiers stood guard on street corners to prevent looting. Some of the soldiers were even attacked and shot at. I, on the other hand, was delighted to see the military, because they were able to restore a semblance of peace and calm to the area. For those who wanted to continue looting and rioting, the soldiers stood in their way and were therefore seen as bad. For the citizens who desired restoration of law and order, the soldiers were seen as good. The former group began to characterize the latter group as racist, and for many the term *law and order* became synonymous with racist attitudes. This is what happens when people begin to polarize themselves based on phrases used by rabble-rousers who for the most part are only interested in their own positions. I think in the long run almost everyone was happy with the performance of the National Guard and with the return to normalcy on the streets of Detroit.

Although racial tensions were explosive in 1967, just one year later the city was a picture of harmony, not because of great political leadership, but rather because the Detroit Tigers were about to win the World Series for the first time in nearly four decades. Everyone was so caught up in the excitement, they forgot their differences and reveled in their common pride. What an incredible testimony to the power of creating common goals and desires—which is, of course, a hallmark of outstanding leadership.

THE STING OF HUMAN NATURE: WHY CAN WE NOT PEACEFULLY COEXIST?

When I was a college student at Yale, the military draft for the Vietnam War was still in effect. People felt that favoritism played a large role in who was selected; therefore, a system was implemented in which a lottery determined who was drafted. All eligible men were assigned a number between 1 and 365, depending on the date of their birth. The lowest numbers were drafted first and the higher numbers were drafted last or not at all. My brother, Curtis, got a very low number and realistically assumed he was going to be drafted, even though he was in college at the time. He decided to at least apply for the military branch of his choice, so he enlisted in the Navy, where he trained as a nuclear atomic submarine operator. I, on the other hand, was dealt lottery number 333, which virtually assured I would not be drafted.

Although I would have readily accepted my responsibility to fight had I been drafted, I found myself wondering why in modern times we are still running around killing each other. Over the course of thousands of years, why has the human race failed to make meaningful strides toward peaceful coexistence? I think the answer is contained in the story of "The Scorpion and the Frog":

A scorpion was trying desperately to reach the opposite bank of a river, but he could not swim. Then he saw a frog swimming leisurely along the shore. He implored the frog to give him a ride on his back to the other side of the river.

"Are you crazy?" the frog said. "Or maybe you think I'm crazy. What would keep you from stinging me, causing me to drown?"

The scorpion answered, "If I sting you while we're in the river, and I cannot swim, I will also drown. Therefore, I have great incentive for keeping you alive."

The frog saw the logic in the scorpion's argument and he agreed to shuttle him across the river on his back. When they reached the deepest part of the river, the frog felt a painful sting on his back. As sensation began to leave his body and he began to sink he asked the scorpion, "Why did you sting me? Now we're both going to die!"

"I'm sorry," the scorpion answered, "but I couldn't help it. You see, it's my nature."

Throughout history, mankind has behaved like the scorpion, and, unfortunately, we can assume that our natural, pugilistic tendencies will persist into the foreseeable future. For that reason, it is important to fortify ourselves against attack and maintain a state-of-the-art military apparatus. Many pacifists among us would strongly disagree, believing that if we are nice to everyone, that everyone will in turn be nice to us, and that peace will reign supreme throughout the world. I would love for that to be true, but in our world pragmatism generally wins out over idealism. I do, however, believe we should continue to work toward the goal of world peace. If we don't set a target, we certainly will not hit it.

Being prepared to protect ourselves does not mean endless expansion of the military budget or insinuating ourselves into every conflict around the globe. One only need look to the history of the Roman Empire to learn significant lessons about what happens when military forces are stretched too thin. The Romans suffered many humiliating losses as a result, which affected the esprit de corps, leading to further erosion of a once fierce fighting force. Also, their need for ever-increasing funding led to burdensome taxes and trumped-up reasons to confiscate private property, particularly that belonging to the wealthy. The loss of a national vision, erosion of morality, and totally irresponsible fiscal policies led to the destruction of what was perhaps the greatest empire the world had ever known. Our nation should keep this in mind when evaluating trouble spots around the world and considering our level of involvement.

There are ways to affect outcomes of such conflicts without investing large amounts of money or engaging the military overtly. I believe it is unwise, however, for us to talk too openly about our political and military objectives because it unnecessarily constrains us and provides our opponents with early warning and the opportunity to prepare. I'm talking about things that have unwisely been criminalized or demonized that are better left undiscussed in a public forum. When dealing with corrupt and evil forces that are bent upon the destruction of our nation, we would be wise to keep them in the dark regarding our intentions and capabilities. For quite some time now, it seems we've lost our grasp on the simple logic in this as we pay too much attention to a vocal, well-meaning, but naïve group of people who insist on transparency in all of our policies. Others will agree with me that integrity and morality are considerably more important than transparency when engaging in military conflicts.

But, some may ask, how are the people to know there is integrity without transparency? Do I have logical, mutually agreeable solutions to satisfy both sides? No. But if the American people know our goals and philosophy, I would expect that they would agree that relating all the details also alerts our enemies. For the sake of our military strategists, soldiers, and the common good, I believe most would be willing to give up a few public details for the sake of better protection.

OUR NATION'S HISTORY FROM ISOLATION TO GLOBAL PARTICIPATION

From the time of its inception until now, the United States has been involved in many military conflicts, but by the early 1900s, we were beginning to be wary of the consequences of war, particularly when there was no direct threat to our nation. While World War I raged, President Woodrow Wilson was determined to maintain US neutrality and allow our economic prosperity to continue. He was strongly supported by his Secretary of State, William Jennings Bryan, many other government officials, and public opinion. But on May 7, 1915, the Lusitania was torpedoed by a German U-boat off the coast of Ireland, killing almost 1,200 people, more than 10 percent of whom were Americans. People around the world expressed great outrage, but particularly in Great Britain and America. Nevertheless, despite sending a series of semi-threatening letters to Germany, President Wilson tried to maintain calm, and discouraged our entry into the war. Although the Germans moderated their U-boat attack policies, US commercial business interests eventually prevailed in advocating war on Germany. America was not prepared for war and contributed little to the effort when we entered in 1917, but by the spring of 1918, very successful recruitment efforts led to the influx of hundreds of thousands of American troops, with more than one million American troops in France by early fall of that year. The Germans, who had been in the driver's seat before the entrance of America, could not match those numbers; therefore, they backed down, and in November of 1918 the Treaty of Versailles was signed, ending the war. Although America was a fledgling superpower in the first part of the twentieth century, it demonstrated great flexibility and cunning military prowess that altered the rest of the world's perception of the US as an isolationist nation, changing the global power dynamics.

After World War I, spurred on by confidence and the tremendous industrial stimulus the war had provided, America enjoyed a thriving business community and unparalleled expansion of the manufacturing sector. We got heavily involved with the international business community, but had little desire to engage in international geopolitical squabbles. Once again, an isolationist mind-set began to prevail, while political tensions throughout Europe, Asia, and Africa began to mount. Our military preparedness had dwindled, even though large conflicts in Asia and Europe were beginning to take place. The Germans were determined to regain their status as a world power, and in 1936 entered into a treaty with Japan, forming the basis for the Axis powers. As the various international conflicts increased, the politically neutral United States sold military, industrial, and nutritional products to supply the war, greatly bolstering its coffers.

There was not unanimous agreement, however, that we should stay out of the war, which had pulled in virtually every world power except the United States. It appears that Franklin D. Roosevelt wanted to get involved, particularly given the friendship he had with Winston Churchill, but our nation's isolationist faction was still too strong. However, on December 7, 1941, Pearl Harbor was attacked by the Japanese, and more than two thousand American servicemen lost their lives. Four days later, the Germans declared war on the United States, and an amazing thing occurred. A spirit of unity encompassed the entire nation, and we went from neutral to strongly committed to the Allied forces overnight.[2]

Prior to our entrance into World War II, many nations of the world had been falling like dominoes before the tyrannical Axis powers, but the Japanese made a strategic error when they awakened the sleeping giant of America. Ours was a nation with the ability to send its young men from the cities, suburbs, and countryside to fight around the world, while sending its young women into factories to build more airplanes, tanks, and mortars than anyone could imagine. Through our industrial might and determination, we became a nation that changed the course of history and delivered the world from brutal tyranny.

The United States and the Soviet Union emerged from World War II as the two superpowers of the world with markedly different philosophies regarding freedom, economics, and geopolitical strategies, which eventually led to the strategic standoff known as the "Cold War." Although it is true that many nations that are free today owe their freedom to the United States, it is also true that we would most likely not have prevailed in *our* quest for freedom from Great Britain in the late 1700s without the help of the French and other nations.

THE FOG OF WAR

In spite of the obvious horrors of World War II for a generation around the world, there were also a number of green shoots that emerged for the United States following that war. National unity and pride was at an all-time high, and our infrastructure for production of industrial goods continued to function very well, leading to a booming post-war economy. The war even helped provide an impetus for the civil rights movement because African-American soldiers had performed so valiantly throughout the conflict. They boasted many heroic ground units as well as the famous Tuskegee Airmen, whose impressive list of successful combat missions is unparalleled. In 1948 President Truman outlawed segregation in the armed forces, paving the way for the abolition of this abominable practice throughout America.

We experienced a similar groundswell of unity after the 9/11 crisis in New York City. Political rancor ceased and almost everyone united behind President George W. Bush for a season. Whether America's ensuing steps into war in Afghanistan and Iraq will be seen as positive or negative remains to be seen, but I can't help thinking there may have been a better way to react that would not have cost us so many lives and financial capital. I believe that if the president had seized the moment and declared that we would become petroleum independent within the next ten years as part of our effort to strip terrorism of its resources, that business, industry, academia, and everyone else would have been foursquare behind him, and we would have been much further ahead in the fight against terrorism than we are today.

First of all, the moderate Arab states would have been terrified about losing their economic base and would most probably have turned Osama bin Laden and anyone else we wanted over on a silver platter immediately. Second, an enormous number of jobs would likely have been created in the process of switching over to a new energy source, and Wall Street would have been booming. Third, the environmentalists would have been ecstatic; and fourth, but most importantly, the terrorists would have been deprived of much-needed funding, which would have gradually strangled their efforts. Oil prices would have fallen dramatically in an attempt to soften our resolve, but good leadership would hopefully have recognized and compensated for such a ploy. The point, of course, is that in some cases clever tactics can be employed outside of military action to respond to hostile actions. A strong military, coupled with wise leadership, will go a long way toward establishing and maintaining peace in the world.

While World War I and World War II had very positive effects on the American economy, subsequent wars have had a neutral effect at best. The

Iraq war should certainly have put an end to the myth that war is good for our economy. It is true that the demand for war products gave the economy a giant boost during our wars largely subsidized by other nations, but today the expense of modern warfare far outweighs any economic benefits it achieves. War is bad on all accounts and should be the very last resort for our nation.

The horrors of war are probably best illustrated by what happened in Hiroshima and Nagasaki at the end of World War II. Not only was there massive destruction of life and property, but the residual effects of radiation after the atomic blast were felt for decades. Although the dropping of atomic weapons certainly hastened the end of the war, the Axis powers were already on the run and their defeat was certain. Nevertheless, the advent of the atomic era forever changed the landscape of large-scale international conflict. One can only imagine what would have happened to the world if the Axis powers had been first to acquire atomic weapons—and one can only imagine what will happen in the future if terrorists are armed with such weapons. A grave responsibility rests with those who are in possession of weapons of mass destruction, and the entire world should endeavor to keep them from rogue nations.

I realize that some feel that the United States and other world powers with nuclear weapons have no right to declare that others cannot have them. On the surface this seems like a fair argument, but can you imagine how many deaths would occur if everyone were given a handgun? Perhaps it would be *fair* to give everyone a handgun, but it certainly would not be *wise*. Although I applaud efforts toward nuclear disarmament, I also realize that if no one had nuclear weapons and one of the madmen of the world acquired them, worldwide tyranny would quickly follow. Therefore, we must be careful in pursuing our goals of an idyllic world.

The next two wars the United States was involved in were really ideological wars. The Korean War was a proxy war, with the Korean Peninsula becoming the site of the first Cold War conflict. It was the first major intervention in the world by the newly formed United Nations, which took action when communist North Korea, backed by China and Russia, invaded South Korea, backed primarily by the United States. The conflict lasted only three years, and Korea remains a divided nation today. In the case of Vietnam, we were trying to stop the spread of communism, which seems like a noble cause to those who hate communism. However, many people love communism, and certainly everyone should have the right to live under the system of their choosing. The problem occurs when a system of government is forcibly imposed upon unwilling participants. It was our attempt to stop such intrusions that led to our participation in these wars. Although our intentions were noble, I question our methodology.

A major question, however, remains: what responsibility does the world's only superpower have when it comes to responding to humanitarian atrocities throughout the world? Should we have intervened in Rwanda to prevent the slaughter of over one million innocent people? Should we have been more concerned about the hundreds of thousands of people Saddam Hussein was slaughtering than the possibility of him possessing weapons of mass destruction? When the United Nations was formed, it was intended to be an international guardian of freedom that would not allow humanitarian atrocities. Like the United States, however, it has become so bogged down in politics that it did virtually nothing to stop these and many other calamities from occurring. Recently, it did vindicate itself to a degree by taking relatively quick action against the ruthless regime of Moammar Gadhafi in Libya, but its overall record leaves something to be desired. These issues become very complex when a nation responds to these atrocities through the lens of such questions as, what's in it for us? and how does it fit into our global strategic goals? They are much simpler to answer, however, when constrained by the principle of doing what's right and moral.

FILLING THE ETHICAL VOID TODAY

A large void in ethical world leadership has been present for quite a while, and this is a perfect time for the United States to step forward and offer effective, morally consistent policies unconstrained by political correctness. If a bully faction or bully nation is beating up on those with whom it disagrees or simply doesn't like, we should immediately stop them with brutal force, if necessary, because it is the right thing to do. If that were done consistently, I guarantee that such incidents would cease almost immediately.

I mention political correctness here because it only hampers effectiveness. For example, a lot of time, effort, and lives were wasted in Fallujah, Iraq, because the terrorists were hiding among the people and using them as shields against the American forces. Political correctness dictates that we cannot kill innocent women and children in the process of destroying the enemy. I certainly agree from a moral perspective, but from a military perspective I would not have played their game. I would have announced via bullhorn and leaflets that in seventy-two hours Fallujah was going to become part of the desert because there were substantial numbers of terrorists hiding there. This would have given people time to flee before the city was destroyed, and is a tactic that would actually save lives not only of women and children, but also men. If the terrorists were foolish enough to choose to remain and to keep people from leaving, any ensuing deaths would clearly be their responsibility. Admittedly these are very bold and definitive steps, but such actions would likely preclude long drawn-out wars, and ultimately decrease the numbers of people killed and injured.

I can just hear pacifists saying, how horrible and brutal—how could a man of God even think such a thing? But they haven't thought beyond their initial reaction. You would not have to take this type of action very often before people began to realize that having terrorists among them was not a good thing, and they would act accordingly to either expose such individuals or expel them. On the surface, this kind of action may seem brutal, but I believe the number of innocent lives that ultimately would be spared is substantial, and it seems to me that it would be more morally acceptable to destroy structures than lives. Buildings can always be replaced, but not so for even one life. When political correctness is not introduced into warfare, efficiency and smart economic policies can prevail.

We have talked about World War I and World War II, but could World War III be in our future? The war on terror has already been declared, and unless we act with courage and decisiveness, there is no question that the terrorists will soon acquire nuclear weapons. Radical Islamic extremists are not satisfied to peacefully coexist with those they consider to be infidels. They feel that such people need to either be converted or destroyed—and there is no middle ground. Although the vast majority of Muslims don't subscribe to this philosophy, they are not very vocal, just as the vast majority of Germans did not subscribe to Hitler's insanity, but instead remained silent, paving the way for some of the most monstrous acts against humanity ever committed. We need to actively combat these extremists in every way possible, including economic warfare. The terrorist network derives most of its money through oil revenues, and we, along with most of the rest of the world, have an insatiable appetite for oil. Unlike the rest of the world, however, we have enormous amounts of oil under North and South Dakota, Montana, and Alaska, as well as offshore oil. I am as much of a conservationist as anyone and love the natural beauty that surrounds us, but the pragmatic part of me warns that there will be no beauty at all if the world is consumed in nuclear conflagration. As we intelligently tap our own resources, we must doggedly pursue other energy sources. With appropriate incentives, I have no question that Americans, with all their ingenuity, can come up with new sources of clean energy in a relatively short period of time.

Providing appropriate incentives to the American people should result in a plethora of ideas and inventions to solve our energy problems. Can you imagine the amount of hydroelectric power alone that is available to us, situated as we are between two oceans? We simply need to invent efficient and inexpensive ways to harness that energy. We also need a way to regulate the way some companies and individuals buy up patents of promising ideas that would threaten their sources of revenue. For instance, petroleum companies should not be allowed to purchase the patent for a new process to harness solar energy. Perhaps no one should be allowed to buy such a patent without demonstrating a clear-cut plan and the capability to bring the plan to fruition. Incorporating such ideas into our society should help America move toward energy independence, leading to greater self-sufficiency and preventing political conflicts over oil.

We have an awesome military with tremendous leadership, and we wisely have civilian oversight of the military. If our leadership is willing to once again return to the moral high ground and use our power to achieve peace and a chance for all to prosper, I believe we will have fulfilled a most noble purpose in the history of our world.

CHAPTER 10

IS HEALTH CARE A RIGHT?

MEDICINE FASCINATED ME AS A CHILD. Whenever a medical story was featured on the television or radio, I was drawn to it. Fueled by my love of books on nature, I was captivated by the life-and-death struggle of animals and insects, and I was also extremely curious when one of our older relatives died about what caused the death. I became convinced as a child of the evils of tobacco and would try to hide the cigarettes of friends and relatives who smoked. I had an insatiable desire to know how things worked, and I was constantly taking things apart (and sometimes reassembling them successfully!). The chemistry set that I received for Christmas when I was eight years old was an endless source of entertainment and learning. All of these things indicated early on that medicine would be an ideal profession for me.

I was particularly intrigued, however, by the stories presented each week in Sabbath School that featured missionary doctors who traveled to remote areas of the world at great personal sacrifice, not only to spread the gospel, but to bring physical healing and reform the health habits of the populace. *What courageous compassion*, I thought, *for them to lay down their lives for others.* Those missionary doctors seemed to me the most noble people on the face of the earth.

In fact, my first public speech, at the age of eight, involved the story of a missionary doctor. It was my turn to give the mission story in the primary division (children aged seven to nine) of our church, and when I told my mother about it, she said, "You should present it as if you were the missionary doctor talking to them."

To do so, I practiced memorizing the story and presenting it dramatically, until I almost convinced myself that I had been there. My mother helped me create a costume the missionary might have worn, and I tried to emulate the speech of an authoritative but compassionate preacher by raising and lowering my voice at the appropriate times in my delivery.

On the morning of my presentation, the children chattered away among themselves, distracted as always, until I began reeling them in with my story. "I was quietly tiptoeing through the jungle in the dark of night without a weapon," I confided to them in a whisper, "knowing that savage warriors had been told to bring me in dead or alive." I fanned a fly away from my face as I pressed on through the imaginary jungle surrounding me.

"Suddenly," I exclaimed, whirling around as I had practiced at home, "a large branch broke behind me." To my joy and amazement, I realized everyone was drawn into the moment with me, and I had my entire audience hooked from there on.

When I finished, the teachers were so enthusiastic they asked me to give the same presentation to the adults the following week, which was unheard of. I refined my presentation over the days that followed, growing ever more nervous as the day approached about performing before a whole church auditorium full of adults. My mother told me I should simply pretend that everyone in the audience was naked—but that did nothing to alleviate my anxiety. Imagining everyone in my church naked was not a pleasant thought!

On Sabbath morning, the stage seemed larger than usual to me. Some of the adults did not look particularly happy to be there, and as I began speaking I initially took refuge behind the large white podium. But as I began to get caught up in the presentation I had practiced so many times, I ventured farther out onto the stage and began whispering and shouting and jumping to the delight of my audience, who applauded loudly when I finished. The adults were incredulous that an eight-year-old could present something so powerfully, and the seed of my public speaking career began to germinate.

After that experience, my desire to be a missionary doctor continued to grow until I was thirteen. By that time I had a much better understanding of what the life of a missionary doctor was like, and the appeal of its lifestyle had dissipated. Perhaps if I had grown up in an environment of economic privilege, I would have pursued my original goal more vigorously, but the thought of a lifetime of continued poverty was something I had a difficult time facing.

By then, however, human behavior and the lives of psychiatrists had captured my attention. The psychiatrists I saw depicted on television seemed like such wise individuals who made a real difference in the lives of desperate people—and to top it off, they drove fancy cars, lived in mansions, and had plush offices. My brother, Curtis, knew of my interest in psychiatry and bought me a subscription to *Psychology Today* for my fourteenth birthday. I really looked forward to receiving my magazine each month, and I became the local amateur psychologist for many of the people around me. I majored in psychology at Yale and took advanced psychiatric courses in medical school at the University of Michigan, fully believing that I was going to become a psychiatrist. However, I was so impressed whenever the neurosurgeons made presentations to our class that I began to have second thoughts about my area of specialization.

So I asked God to give me wisdom to make a proper decision that would have a lifetime of implications. I truly believe God gives everyone special gifts and talents, and as I began to assess mine, I quickly realized that the talents necessary to be a good neurosurgeon—good eye-hand coordination, steadiness, calmness, and the ability to think in three dimensions—were all things I possessed already. After realizing that, the decision for me was quite easy, and I have never regretted it. When I made that decision to become a neurosurgeon, I did briefly think about the fact that I would have a much smaller impact on the lives of people than I would have had as a missionary doctor, but I felt that God was leading me and that he clearly knew more than I did about his plans for me. As it turns out, because of the amazing career that he orchestrated for me, I have been able to touch more lives through my books, magazine articles, interviews, and a made-for-television movie than perhaps I could have as a missionary doctor. It was that very ability to positively touch lives that attracted me to medicine in the first place—and is the reason that many of our nation's doctors, nurses, and other health-care professionals are attracted to the field as well.

PRIVATE DECISIONS, PUBLIC CONSEQUENCES?

When I was a neurosurgery resident at Johns Hopkins, on numerous occasions my wife and I would be in the car driving and suddenly a motorcyclist with no helmet on would whiz past us, seemingly without a care in the world. I had to fight feelings of anger as I thought about how often I was awakened at two in the morning to respond to a severe head trauma case from a motorcyclist who was not wearing a helmet involved in a motor vehicle accident. Yet that motorcyclist had every right to neglect his own safety, and at that time, that right was protected by law.

Subsequently, helmet laws were enacted, much to the displeasure of many motorcyclists, but to the great relief of many health-care practitioners. The ramifications of such irresponsible behavior on behalf of the motorcyclists, however, extend far beyond the inconvenience suffered by people like me who had to take care of them. Sometimes the head injuries were very severe, and saving the victims became an extremely expensive process that involved not only acute medical care, but also long-term rehabilitative services, and in some very sad cases, chronic maintenance for those with little or no chance of resuming productive lives. Although doctors sometimes resent having to give up time with their families and the many other sacrifices associated with the medical profession, few people stop to philosophize about whether the victims have a right to consume enormous amounts of medical resources. In our society, we do not discuss the behavior that created the problem, and we generally do not discuss the price of treatment or the significant impact on their family and societal resources (welfare).

Not many years ago, when I was on call, a fifteen-year-old boy was brought into our pediatric emergency room with a high fever and a decreasing level of consciousness. After a rapid and thorough workup, we discovered that he had multiple intracranial bacterial abscesses. It took several operations and extended time in the intensive care unit to get his health temporarily under control. Saving him cost hundreds of thousands of dollars, and in the end he had no insurance or other means to pay his bill. We subsequently discovered that he was in the country illegally, but that did not change the fact that he was in dire need of medical care.

We do not like to ask questions in situations such as this that force us to make judgments about who should get care and how much care they should get. It is far easier to simply render whatever treatment is necessary and let someone else worry about the bill. In America, we tend to have a very negative reaction to the health-care systems of countries such as England that are based on a socialized model. And we particularly abhor the rationing of care based on such factors as age.

For example, under some socialized systems, kidney transplants are not even considered for individuals over the age of sixty, which means that most of our United States Supreme Court justices would be too old to be considered for such a life-saving treatment in many countries with socialized medicine. Who is right? Those who feel that it is our moral obligation to treat everyone regardless of cost, or those who feel that rationing and other means of cost containment make more sense to our nation's health-care funding in the long run. As with virtually all controversial issues, the answer usually lies somewhere in between, and compromise can be very helpful. I must admit that in my many years of medicine, I have never witnessed a patient abandoned because of lack of money. In America we suffer much more from a lack of money than we do from a lack of compassion.

THERE'S NO SUCH THING AS A FREE ~~LUNCH~~ HEALTH-CARE POLICY

One of the by-products of our society's strong value on compassion is the development of an entitlement mentality among large portions of our populace. I have noticed at Johns Hopkins Hospital that many of the indigent patients — instead of feeling grateful for the fact that people are willing to extend to them sophisticated and expensive care with little or no remuneration — are the most belligerent and the most likely to initiate lawsuits. By no stretch of the imagination are all indigent patients like this — and I shouldn't even have to make such a disclaimer — but there exists in our society today a vocal and highly sensitive minority who are constantly monitoring every word to try to find fault with the finer points, rather than examining the overall message and attempting to engage in constructive dialogue to help find solutions. The fact that some of these patients become abusive and threatening does nothing to improve their care and actually is destructive to the development of the kinds of relationships with nurses, doctors, and other health-care providers that ensure quality care. No one likes to be around those always looking to pick a fight, which means that a belligerent person or their child might not be checked on and chatted with as frequently as someone who is reasonable and pleasant to be around. That, of course, means something might be missed, which continues to exacerbate the doctor-patient relationship.

Contrary to popular belief, one of the reasons many physicians refuse to see indigent patients is not that they cannot pay, but because of the poor treatment they receive from such patients. This cycle can then lead to degenerating doctor-patient relationships and a higher frequency of lawsuits. Care of the indigent has always been a big part of medicine in America, as it should be, but it should be seen as charitable work as opposed to mandatory labor. As a society, we could even explore certain incentives for health-care workers to engage in even more charitable work.

Our first child, Murray, was born in Australia, and though he has dual citizenship with the United States, he was officially an Aussie first. The health-care system in Australia provides substantial benefits for its citizens, and when a baby is born, the family receives a "baby bonus," which provides substantial income throughout childhood. There was also a "milk allowance" and free nursing care centers for babies. Basic medical care was provided for all citizens at no cost, but everyone had the right to purchase private health insurance, which enabled subscribers to enjoy more personalized services and less waiting time. Although it was a two-tiered system, I did not witness much resentment by those receiving their basic care free of charge against those who could afford private insurance. There may be some substantial lessons that we can learn from such a system.

For instance, everyone has different needs and we do not have to have a cookie-cutter, one-size-fits-all system. Because one person drives a Chevrolet and another drives a Mercedes, it doesn't automatically mean that the Chevrolet driver is deprived or needs some supplement. The fact is, he can get to the same places as a Mercedes driver with perhaps slightly less comfort. People have different medical needs and some can afford the Chevrolet plan while others can afford the Mercedes plan. We should leave it at that and not try to micromanage people's lives as long as the care is adequate.

Not long ago, as I was writing in a patient's chart at the Johns Hopkins Children's Center, I overheard two female housekeeping staff members complaining about the fact that they had to shell out five to ten dollars as a co-pay every time they saw their doctor. It was grossly unjust, they felt, for anyone to expect them to use their meager salaries to contribute to paying their health-care costs. I started to ask them whether they thought medical care should be completely free—and who should be responsible to cover the cost of the free program. I did not want to embarrass them, and so I did not press the issue, but that conversation underscores widespread attitudes in our society today. Those ladies are not bad people, and they do their jobs very well, but they are totally misinformed about health-care financing and the implications of a nation perpetuating irresponsible medical fiscal policies. As long as everyone is concerned solely with their own good, equitable health care for everyone will be impossible.

Our founding fathers felt that everyone had a right to life, liberty, and the pursuit of happiness—but does everyone have a right to health care? The Bible tells us that almost every time Jesus arrived in a new area, he first healed the sick. These acts of his provided goodwill and credibility, making it much easier for him to talk about the weightier matters of life. Perhaps the lesson for us is to make sure that the basic needs of the most helpless among us are taken care of. Maybe the real question is not whether health care should be available to everyone in our society, but rather how can we provide universal health care in an efficient and cost-effective way.

I have to chuckle when politicians talk about ways to acquire more money to fund solutions to our health care, for we already spend close to twice as much money per capita on health care as the next closest nation in the world. The problem is not *allocation* of money, but rather how it is *spent*. If other nations can spend half as much or less and still achieve good basic health care for every one of their citizens, our system must be filled with waste and abuse. Perhaps it was the recognition of this fact that led to massive attempts to reform health care in this nation by the Obama administration. I'm very happy that our politicians are paying attention to this overwhelming problem, but I am less happy about the solutions that have been forced upon the populace. Perhaps well-meaning individuals temporarily forgot that we live in a nation where the majority does not impose its will on the minority simply because it can. Perhaps the better approach is to take a step back and analyze our health-care situation, then apply logic.

THE "SAUDI ARABIAN SOLUTION"

In having an appendectomy in Detroit versus having one in, say, Miami versus having one in New York City, you will find there are myriad different ways that your health-care provider must submit your bill and collect payment. Unfortunately, our health-care insurance system has become so complex that virtually all medical offices and larger practices need billing specialists just to navigate its intricacies. All of this variation and complexity produces mountains of paperwork and requires armies of people to push it around. Funding all these workers causes a larger portion of your health-care dollars to go toward paying administrative costs than the portion that goes to pay the actual professional fees; in fact, about twice as much goes to paper pushers. Imagine how much money we could save if we had a consistent and simplified system for medical billing and collections. Interestingly, every single medical diagnosis carries a designation known as the ICD–9 code, and every single medical procedure has a designation known as a CPT code. If we created uniform payments for the codes, all bills could be submitted very easily electronically into one common computer system, with virtually instant payment from the insurance companies.

Of course there are always special-interest groups that fight simplification of anything because they benefit from the complexities. In this case, the insurance companies would almost certainly object to such a system, arguing that some unscrupulous doctors would simply submit "evidence" that they had done two appendectomies instead of one and instantly receive payment for two. The insurance companies would claim that, without layers of oversight, the potential for massive fraud would be enormous. Another special-interest group that would likely resist would consist of doctors living in areas where reimbursement is traditionally higher than in the rest of the country. They would certainly not be eager to relinquish their financial advantage.

First of all, as someone who has been in the field of medicine my entire professional life, I can tell you with great certainty that there are very few physicians who would engage in that type of fraud, but there certainly are some. However, the solution for dealing with those few is not to create a gigantic and expensive bureaucracy as we have done, but rather to apply what I term the "Saudi Arabian solution." Why don't people steal very often in Saudi Arabia? Obviously because the punishment is the amputation of one or more fingers. I would not advocate chopping off people's limbs, but there would be some very stiff penalties for this kind of fraud, such as loss of one's medical license for life, no less than ten years in prison, and loss of all of one's personal possessions. Not only would this be a gigantic deterrent to fraud, but to protect themselves every physician in practice would check every single bill quite thoroughly before submitting it, which would not be that difficult to do and document.

As for the physicians who live in areas where they are more highly compensated, they would simply have to adjust just like everyone else in society has to during lean times. If there was no difference in payments based on location, you would see specialists disperse from those highly paid areas to other areas throughout the country, which would be wonderful for the nation in terms of access to quality care. This migration of top specialists to other areas of the country is unlikely to affect the quality of care in the large metropolises and would probably even be beneficial because there would be less competition for patients and fewer unnecessary procedures being done in order to stay busy.

When there are too many specialists in one region, it is not uncommon for diseases to be overtreated by those specialists, who all like to be kept busy. The same thing occurs when there are too many medical centers. Everyone wants to be seen as the premier medical center, offering all the latest treatments and technologies. Thus you have massive duplication of medical services, again with an intense desire for all of them to be maximally utilized. It makes a great deal more sense to have each of the medical centers in the same region designated to specialize in only certain areas, with the others taking up the slack. For example, one could serve as the cardiac center, while another serves as the neuroscience center, and yet another could be the renal center.

In order to make a system like this work, reasonable, consistent, and timely payment must be a given. Compensation has to be fair given the investment of time and money necessary to acquire the skills to render good medical care. Compensation cannot be determined by insurance companies, who make more money by elbowing their way in as the middleman and confiscating as much of the transaction between patient and caregiver as they can. It might be smart to couple physician reimbursement to that for lawyers. I say this jokingly because, as everyone knows, lawyers are unlikely to allow their compensation to be reduced by arbitrary outside forces. Physicians generally are not going to fight for themselves, however, which is why it is so easy to take advantage of them, but that certainly is not the case for lawyers. With appropriate time and effort, I am confident that we can come up with an equitable system to take advantage of the ICD–9 codes, the CPT codes, and computer systems, saving ourselves hundreds of billions of dollars a year that could be used to shore up Medicare or provide for the indigent.

INSURANCE COMPANIES SQUEEZING OUT THOSE WHO NEED IT MOST

When I first became an attending physician many years ago, our ability to take care of indigent patients was far greater than it is today. Almost all physicians voluntarily devoted a portion of their practice to the poor and indigent, fully recognizing that this represented a financial loss for them. At that time, however, reimbursement from insurance companies was much better than it is today, and our profit margin made charitable care possible and even fun.

Today, to a large extent, insurance companies call the shots on what they want to pay, to whom, and when. Consequently, even busy doctors operate with a very slim profit margin and find it much more difficult to offer care to the poor and pay for it out of their profit. I speak from personal experience because over the last many years, I have had to cut my staff significantly due to low insurance company reimbursements. That cut in staff also means a cut in services that we can offer. Our desire to help more people is at odds with our ability to do so, due to lack of funding. Although I could donate my services, I cannot volunteer the services of my operating room staff or other ancillary personnel to help care for a patient who can't afford their own medical care.

This is an ideal place for the intervention of government regulators who, with the help of medical professionals, could establish fair and consistent remuneration throughout the country. To accomplish this, essentially all of the insurance companies would have to become non-profit service organizations with standardized, regulated profit margins. I should quickly add that this is not the paradigm that I see for all businesses, and in fact this is uniquely appropriate for the health-insurance industry, which deals with people's lives and quality of existence. These things should not be treated like commodities or industrial products. That may sound radical, but is it as radical as allowing a company to increase its profits by denying care to sick individuals? In the long run this would also be good for the insurance companies, who could then concentrate on providing good service to their customers, rather than focusing on under-cutting their competitor and increasing their profit margin. It would also drastically decrease the number of people each insurance company would have to hire, all of whom have to be paid out of the health-care dollar. Thus insurance premiums would decline, making health insurance more affordable for everyone.

A HEALTH STAMP PROGRAM?

But what about those who have no health-care insurance? How are we supposed to care for them when we are already stretched to our financial limits? Interestingly enough, there aren't, in fact, 52 million people without health-care insurance in this country[1] — all they have to do is go to the emergency room where by law they must be taken care of if they truly have an emergency. The problem is, emergency care costs five times as much as it would if they were getting regular preventive care in a clinic. And, unfortunately, the rest of us pay for it. The logical question we should ask then is, how do we get those same people to go to the clinic instead?

First of all, we must recognize that we are already paying for their care at a much higher rate when they show up in the emergency room. If we can get them to go to the clinic, however, we will still be paying for their health care, but at a much lower rate. We might do well to look at another government program that has been around for decades and saved millions of people from chronic hunger. The food stamp program allocates money for food in an electronic account at the beginning of each month. People learn very quickly not to go out the first five days and buy porterhouse steak, leaving them with nothing to spend on food for the rest of the month. They learn to look for bargains and other ways to stretch their allocation for the entire month. If we had electronic medical accounts for the indigent in this country, they too would have incentive to save money when medical problems arose. For example, if Mr. Smith has a diabetic foot ulcer and goes to the emergency room, he will be adequately patched up and sent out—but if he goes to the clinic, not only will he be paying much less, but he will be patched up and an attempt will be made to get his diabetes under control, hopefully preventing a trip back in three weeks with another diabetic complication.

By looking at preventive care and wellness, we as a society will begin to save enormous amounts of money while achieving a significantly higher level of health. This is especially important as our population continues to age, since aging is accompanied by a slew of medical problems that can be avoided or reduced if detected early. Also, I am very fond of saying that if everyone ate three well-balanced meals each day, drank eight glasses of water or water-equivalent substances, regularly got a full night's sleep, regularly exercised, and did not smoke or put harmful substances into their bodies, we in the medical profession would become very bored. Unfortunately, given the state of health in our nation, I don't think we have to worry about that anytime soon.

BRINGING DOWN THE COST OF HEALTH CARE

Often when people are looking for a new job, they're very interested in the health-care benefits that are offered. Because health-care insurance has become so expensive, most people are not able to afford it on their own and therefore need to be sure that their employer includes this as a benefit. But *why* is health-care insurance so expensive?

Much of the expense is due to coverage of catastrophic medical events. There was a time when premature babies or babies with significant birth defects simply died, which cost the insurance company very little. Now, however, thanks to developments in medical technology, we're able to put such babies in incubators and treat them, usually saving their lives—but then we hand the insurance company a bill for $1 million. We can take an eighty-five-year-old woman with diabetes, hypertension, and thyroid disease who develops a brain tumor or cardiac condition, and successfully treat her, and then give the insurance company a bill for a few hundred thousand dollars. This kind of scenario, repeated on a regular basis, drove insurance companies to drastically increase their premiums, resulting in the situation we have today. I certainly applaud all the medical advances that have length-ened all of our lives while giving us quality of life, but there must be a logical solution to the ever-rising cost of insurance premiums.

One solution would be to remove from the insurance companies the responsibility for catastrophic health-care coverage, making it a government responsibility. I can hear someone shouting now that the government can never do anything correctly, but I beg to differ. It is because of a government program known as FEMA (Federal Emergency Management Agency) that most of us are able to afford our homeowners insurance. If there were no FEMA, Allstate, State Farm, Nationwide, and all the other homeowner insurance companies would be telling us that they had to drastically increase premiums because there might be an earthquake, tornado, hurricane, tsunami, or other natural disaster that would otherwise drain their coffers. Homeowners' insurance would be so expensive that you would have to ask your employer to cover it.

Clearly, if the health-care insurance companies did not have to cover catastrophic health care, it would be relatively easy by analyzing actuarial tables to determine how much money they are likely to be liable for each year, which of course would determine how much money they had to take in. With this information at our disposal, health insurance companies could be regulated just as utilities are regulated. If we did not regulate utilities, few people would be able to afford their water or electricity.

The next question, of course, is, how will the government pay for catastrophic health care? This is open for debate, but I think it would be quite reasonable to allow insurance companies a 15 percent annual profit, 5 percent of which would go to the government's national catastrophic health-care fund. Since the government would now have the responsibility of paying for catastrophic health care, we as a society would be forced to examine the policies that have led to a situation in which 40 to 50 percent of all health-care dollars are spent during the last six months of a person's life. We put dying people in intensive care units while testing, poking, and prodding them until they render up their last breath. Unlike most other countries of the world, many of us do not seem to acknowledge that death is not optional. It is perfectly reasonable to send terminal patients to hospice, where compassionate and comfortable care can be rendered until death takes place. Much of the excessive care that currently occurs when a patient is terminal is given by health-care providers who fear lawsuits if they fail to provide that care. Others are simply procedure-oriented, recognizing that they will be paid whether the patient survives or not. Fortunately, these individuals are relatively rare in the medical profession. Again, I can hear some people screaming after reading this that I am advocating for "death panels." Some people like to put forth terms like this because they stir up emotional responses rather than encouraging people to engage in rational dialogue aimed at resolving issues. Obviously, as our population ages and as our medical technology becomes more sophisticated and expensive, the potential for bankrupting our society with medical costs skyrockets.

We are facing a time when we have to be pragmatic, while at the same time exercising compassion. One day, we will be able to keep the average person alive for 150 or even 200 years due to medical advances, and we will then be faced with the question, should we use our advanced knowledge in a way that will rapidly overpopulate the world? The emotional answer would be, yes, of course, we should use our knowledge to extend every life, and we can worry about the consequences later. A more rational response would include examining the effect on the entire population of such action and perhaps advocating a more measured course of action.

I remember a case of a prominent individual who had been in an automobile accident and was rendered a C−1 quadriplegic, which means not only was he paralyzed from the neck down, but he could not breathe without assistance. We could have made the decision to keep him alive at all costs, but through a unique system of communication that we were able to work out with him, he indicated that he wanted to die. After much debate, we yielded to his wishes and withdrew ventilatory support. In the long run, I think our course of action was both compassionate and pragmatic. If we integrate compassion and logic into our decision-making processes, I am convinced that we will deal with newly emerging ethical dilemmas appropriately.

When I was a member of the President's Council on Bioethics, discussions on matters such as these were very complex, but they need to be engaged in now to avoid a reactive situation in the future. I believe age should not be the determining factor of the level of care that should be given. Rather we should consider a person's potential for quality long-term survival. Many people in their eighties and nineties are very productive members of society, and they certainly should not be denied insurance coverage for certain procedures simply because of age alone. Approaching these problems with logic rather than with emotion leading us will yield the right answers, but it will require in-depth discussions by wise people. As the Bible says, "In the multitude of counsellors there is safety" (Proverbs 11:14).

When a society faces major changes, such as drastically increased life expectancy, its people should examine the effects of such a change and make logical, appropriate adjustments. We should thoroughly examine the effects of our aging society on our way of life and devise compassionate methods of easing the burden of aging both on the individual and the family.

PRODUCING AND PROTECTING OUR HEALTH-CARE DOLLARS

"The only thing that prevents us from having the most fabulous health-care packages imaginable for every citizen of the United States is lack of money," some may say. How can we get more money to invest in health care? Perhaps, as some have suggested, we can simply tax the rich since they have plenty and should be willing to share with everyone. Another idea—which now perhaps seems radical, but once was a pillar of the American way—is to grow the economy, providing a lift for every segment of society.

Consider the following story to illustrate: There once were two brothers, each of whom got married, had children, and moved to separate deserted islands. Their diet consisted solely of trees, and they could eat every part of the tree, including the roots, bark, branches, and leaves. The family of one of the brothers always monitored the new growth of trees and anxiously devoured every tender sapling, which of course never allowed them to grow into mature trees. Eventually, that family ate every sapling on the island and died of starvation. The other family was very disciplined and—while they ate some of the trees—allowed most of the saplings to grow into mature trees, providing them with unlimited food forever.

This is a simple story, but it is easy to see how it applies to a government that continues to tax the rich until there are no more rich, and then begins to tax everyone else without ever curbing its growth or its appetite for money. Eventually it destroys itself. A much wiser government in need of money would examine the methods used by the rich to obtain their wealth and would try to create an economic environment that would cultivate even more rich people, all of whom would pay their fair share of taxes, vastly increasing the government's coffers. In other words, the more productive people you have in your society, the bigger your tax base, and if those people are paying their proportionate share based on income, it will be a big win for the government. All we have to do is study our nation's own history of entrepreneurial innovation[2] to understand what needs to be done to rev up our economy once again.

Generating more money to go toward our nation's health care also requires protecting the money we have—and we lose tens of billions of dollars to Medicare and Medicaid fraud every year. This is something we have not been able to control, either because we don't care very much and view other issues as much more important, or because we are incompetent. Both of these problems we can fix, which gives me hope that we will not forever be robbed. If we are ever going to have adequate funding for health care and other major line items in our budget, however, we have to put an end to waste and fraud throughout the government, and we must create a friendly climate for economic growth.

These are such basic, commonsense ideas, I have a hard time understanding why so many of our government officials totally lack insight on this. I have heard important people in Washington say that fraud, waste, and abuse are an integral part of our system of government and that there is really nothing to be done about it. I hope and pray that we have not fallen to accepting the very things our founding fathers so desperately wanted to avoid. We cannot capitulate to moral decay, and our history dictates that we should not give up this fight.

It is extremely difficult to estimate how much money is wasted in the health-care arena because doctors engage in defensive medicine to avoid lawsuits. During the health-care debate prior to the passage of the bill in 2010, many opponents of tort reform said that adding that to the health-care bill would only save us in the neighborhood of $5 billion a year. That $5 billion is nothing to sneeze at, but I think the savings would be much greater than that. Many more tests and procedures are ordered than are needed to bolster the defense in case of a lawsuit. My wife and I were at a public forum in Virginia during the fall before the health-care law was voted on and one of the speakers was Dr. Howard Dean, whose campaign for president some years ago famously ended with a wild scream. I do not agree with many of his political views, but he is an honest individual as far as politicians go. Someone asked him the question, "Why is tort reform not included in the health-care bill?"

"It's really quite simple," he replied. "The Trial Lawyers Association gives us [the Democratic Party] a great deal of money, and they don't want it in there."

Many people in the audience were shocked at his candor. He only said what many of us knew was true, but very few in the Democratic Party were willing to admit it. As a neurosurgeon, which is one of the two most-sued specialties, I have witnessed many lawsuits against doctors that destroyed careers, confidence, and families when the doctor had done nothing wrong. Unfortunately, in many such cases a patient suffered an unfortunate outcome, even though everyone was trying extremely hard to solve the problem. In our country there is no way to recoup lost income, lost potential, or other losses, including emotional distress, other than filing a lawsuit against the health-care provider or the hospital.

Most other countries have figured out a way to take care of injured individuals by providing some form of redress, but our great nation simply has no clue how to solve this problem. Obviously that's not true, and like almost everything else in our nation that doesn't make any sense politically, a special interest group is heavily involved behind the scenes. In this case, it's the Trial Lawyers Association. As long as we continue to empower and submit to the influence of special interest groups, nothing we do will ever make sense or benefit the general populace.

By dealing with the problems I've discussed in this chapter, we could reduce the cost of our health-care insurance to the point that most individuals and families could afford to own their own policies. This would provide portability between health-care providers (limiting exclusions for preexisting conditions) and the potential to further reduce health-care premiums for those with healthy lifestyles. For instance, if people owned their own policy, a premium reduction could be offered for anyone having an annual physical examination. We would detect many medical problems during the early stages of development, when treatment is much easier and less expensive. Also, if the patient owns his or her own health-care policy, the doctor would not likely order excessive testing without being questioned about it, since doing so could impact the patient's premiums. A fiduciary relationship would develop between the doctor and patient since there is no detached third party receiving the bills — and that, of course, would result in tremendous savings. In other words, your doctor's responsibility would shift from what is required by the insurance company to what is medically and financially good for you, the patient. Also, if people owned their own health-care policies, they would not have to relinquish them when they turned sixty-five, which might alleviate some of the pressure on Medicare. These are only a few of many ideas to solve our health-care crisis.

As we continue to try to improve health-care access and quality for everyone, we might do well to ask ourselves the question, if the Golden Gate Bridge fell down, who would we get to rebuild it — structural engineers or people who like to talk about building bridges? In like fashion, we would be wise to put health-care reform in the hands of the people who know the most about health care — those providing the care and those receiving it.

— CHAPTER 11—

A NATION DIVIDED

GROWING UP IN BOSTON AND DETROIT, I had political views that largely reflected those of the adults around me. Family, friends, and neighbors generally felt that they had been oppressed and that the responsibility for redressing these injustices rested with the government or with others. By the time I reached high school, the civil rights movement was in full swing, and the Democratic Party was positioning itself as the champion of civil rights. Like most young black people, I accepted the label of Democrat and endeavored to be a part of that struggle. After President Kennedy was assassinated and Lyndon B. Johnson took over, a host of social programs were unleashed, aimed at helping oppressed minorities and people like us living in poverty. I was particularly thrilled with Johnson's "War on Poverty," which I thought would significantly improve our family's lifestyle. Even though my mother worked very hard cleaning other people's houses, we still benefitted from government commodities such as cheese and flour. We also received food stamps and bus tokens. Even though she was not a welfare mom, my mother still very much appreciated the government assistance we did receive from time to time. Still, I had an inherent dislike for government assistance and was frankly quite embarrassed that we had to accept anything from them.

By the time I entered college at Yale University, I was running away from poverty and didn't want to discuss that part of my life with anyone. But neither did I identify with the wealth on constant display at Yale. At that time in my life, I was proud to see groups such as the Black Panthers standing up to brutal police tactics, and though I never joined any radical student organizations, I kept abreast of the activities of the Students for a Democratic Society (SDS), the Weathermen, and other groups willing to use aggressive tactics to accomplish "social justice." When George McGovern became the Democratic nominee to run for president of the United States, I voted for him enthusiastically along with multitudes of young people, all of us looking forward to a utopian world of peace and love. We envisioned it as a world without war, racism, or poverty. Plenty of hippies and flower children around me smoked pot, used illicit drugs, and engaged in free love as part of that utopian dream.

Because of my love of God and my religious upbringing, I didn't become involved in sex or drugs, but I still identified strongly with the antiwar protesters and the revolutionaries. I was quite unhappy when George McGovern was soundly defeated by Richard Nixon in 1972 and it looked as if life would go on as usual. I was a senior in college at the time and starting to think more about medical school than social justice.

When I entered medical school the following fall, I immersed myself deeply in my studies and paid little attention to the political scene. The first year of medical school required a significant lifestyle adjustment in order to master so much material. There was not a lot of compassion for students who fell behind, and I saw many of my friends' hopes and dreams shattered by the merciless monster of academia.

As I struggled early on, my academic advisor strongly suggested that I forget about medical school and pursue another area of study. Fortunately I ignored his advice and redoubled my efforts to succeed. It meant getting up at 6 a.m. and studying constantly until 11 p.m. six days a week, only taking off the Sabbath in order to recharge my batteries. That intensive effort not only salvaged my academic career, but allowed me to flourish and begin to earn top grades and respect from teachers and students alike. Although I was still a Jimmy Carter Democrat, I was starting to sympathize with people who advocated for personal responsibility and self-reliance, since those were the traits largely responsible for my success in medical school.

By the time I began training as a neurosurgical resident at Johns Hopkins, I began paying attention to politics again and was particularly intrigued by the optimistic speeches of Jimmy Carter versus the no-nonsense, very practical—although sometimes harsh—speeches of Ronald Reagan. Although Reagan's logical approach to many of our social and international problems appealed to me, he was a Republican. Because of my bias in favor of the Democratic Party, I figured Reagan must, by definition, be greedy, selfish, and callous toward the poor.

As I got to know more Republicans and conservatives, however, I came to realize that many of my political beliefs were based on nothing other than propaganda, and that there were just as many decent Republicans as there were decent Democrats. I found that it was the Republicans who were responsible for the abolition of slavery and for the passage of the Civil Rights Act. I also began to realize that it was not political biases that were largely responsible for the plight of African-Americans in our nation, but rather racist attitudes. After the many gains realized through the civil rights movement, racist people from *both* parties adopted a paternalistic attitude toward African-Americans and enacted federal and state programs designed to take care of people who couldn't take care of themselves—people who were ignorant, stupid, or just plain lazy. In the process of being "do-gooders," both Republicans and Democrats removed much of the drive and determination from innumerable African-Americans, who found it easier to accept government charity than continue on a path of hard work and self-reliance. Once people learn that their irresponsible behavior, such as having babies that they cannot care for, results in larger paychecks from the government, those lifestyle choices have negative implications for the entire nation for generations to come. Any attempt to withdraw government charity is seen as a heartless attack upon the most vulnerable members of our society. Most of the national media had aligned themselves with those involved in the civil rights struggle, which was the right thing to do. Unfortunately, most of the media also failed to recognize the long-term harm caused by those with good intentions who were robbing poor families of the incentive to obtain the American dream through their own efforts.

This kind of smothering political "compassion" that skewed the mindset of large segments of our nation's populace after the gains of the civil rights movement reminds me of the problems facing Yellowstone National Park in the 1950s. Many tourists, full of good intentions, were eager to feed the bears, who were very cute in their antics to encourage visitors to hand over food. The bears quickly lost their fear of people, and instead of hunting for their traditional prey, they began invading camps and breaking into cars and campers looking for food. The forest rangers quickly realized they had a major problem on their hands, one that endangered the tourists' lives. The park enacted rules forbidding feeding of the bears, which exacerbated the situation acutely for a while. But through brilliant management, the bear population relearned how to fend for themselves and began to stay away from the people.

I am not equating people to animals, of course, but rather simply making the point that it is quite easy to become accustomed to an easier way of life, and after a while to believe that one has a *right* to that easier way of life. As I witnessed this happening decades ago throughout our nation, however, I came to believe that we were robbing people of their dignity and the desire to support themselves. Even though I ultimately voted for Jimmy Carter both in 1976 and 1980, my political views were gradually shifting, and by 1984, those views were much more consistent with Ronald Reagan's and those of the Republican Party. I was particularly disenchanted with the extreme partisanship of the Democratic Party at the time, which drove me even further toward the right. Then, when the Monica Lewinsky scandal broke in 1997, I witnessed the extreme partisan politics coming from the Republican Party, which I equally detested. It was quite clear to me that *both* parties needed to re-examine their values, or lack thereof.

Over the years, I found that no political party really represented my views of fairness, decency, and adherence to the principles set forth by the United States Constitution in 1787. So I became a registered Independent and have remained so until this day. I hope and pray that someday politicians on both sides of the aisle will learn to work together and not see each other as mortal enemies. Working toward compromise to solutions for the common good of the people is the only way that our leaders will be able to solve the enormous problems faced by our nation.

The lives of some close friends of ours were destroyed due to lack of compromise. The husband felt that he had a special gift of singing and used a great deal of the family's resources to pay for voice lessons. The wife was in the health-care profession and worked overtime to take care of the family needs, and she strongly disagreed with the way her husband was "squandering" the money. In his opinion, however, he was "investing" in a wonderful future. They were unable to resolve their differences, and one night I was awakened by a phone call informing me that the husband, wife, and one of their children had been killed in an accident. The wife, very distraught, had been driving very fast and had plowed the car into the back of a tractor-trailer truck, killing everyone. This needless tragedy could have been avoided if all were in a better frame of mind, willing to have some reasonable give-and-take. In the same way, many of the problems facing our nation today could be resolved if only the two sides were able to reason together and compromise when necessary.

FINGER-POINTING FUTILITY

When constructive compromise on the part of both political parties is supplanted with a winner-takes-all battle of wills, the wheels of US progress seize up. And when our leaders refer to members of the opposite party as "enemies" one minute and then proclaim how important it is to have civil discourse and cooperation the next minute, it is not hard to understand why people become hardened to anything a politician says these days. But perhaps skepticism toward our leadership suggests we are close to returning to the founders' original intent of limited government and more local, individual responsibility. As a result, politicians would become less important to our country's direction, government would become smaller, and people would step back into the role of taking charge of their own lives. It may seem like a pipe dream, but I truly believe it is possible.

We frequently hear it said that hatred among voters and politicians alike toward the opposite political party is worse today than it has ever been. But a careful reading of historical documents, including political commentaries and cartoons, shows that the differences between what were known as the Federalist Party and the Democratic-Republican Party were every bit as intense — if not more so — in the days of Alexander Hamilton than what we see today. Some of those philosophical differences, in fact, eventually led to the fatal duel in which Hamilton was murdered by Burr.

Because we now have twenty-four-hour news cycles and cable channels, we have constant analysis of political bickering by mostly partisan correspondents and pundits. Even if the Democrats and Republicans were not enemies, many news agencies profit from the controversy by constantly stoking the flames of disagreements. Unfortunately, Democrats and Republicans today *do* appear to be mortal enemies, much to the detriment of our country. The vitriol hurled across the aisle from both parties is staggering, yet they both seem totally incapable of looking in the mirror and recognizing their own hypocrisy. When the party becomes more important than principle, we are in dire straits, for it reveals that our leaders are incapable or unwilling to think critically for themselves. No two people should think exactly alike on all issues, even if they are members of the same party, because people have different experiences that have shaped their lives and their perspectives.

THE BEAUTY OF DIVERSITY

I recently attended a rather elegant dinner party in Washington, DC, and had an opportunity to speak at length with Republican Senator Scott Brown of Massachusetts. I told him how much I admired the fact that over the past several months he had been the object of scorn by both Democrats *and* Republicans because his votes are based on his principles and beliefs rather than on the party line. If everyone in the United States Senate voted that way, I believe we would all be shocked by how rational and reasonable the bills would be coming out of the congressional chambers. Unfortunately, the polarity we see in Democratic and Republican stands on issues suggests that many of our representatives have become puppets of their political party. All voters would be wise to look at their representatives' voting records to see if they agree with their views or whether they are always consistent with the party view. If your views and their views coincide the vast majority of the time and the areas where they do not coincide are not deal breakers, then this is likely someone who represents you well. If, on the other hand, you find major disagreements with your point of view, you should do the responsible thing, which is to vote for the person who represents your views regardless of party affiliation. If we all made a concerted effort to do this, I believe we would be delighted with Congress and their actions instead of having a congressional body with an approval rating of less than 20 percent.

The strength and unity of our nation was severely threatened by secessionists in the mid-1800s, those who wanted to form the Confederate States of America in the South to maintain the practice of slavery as a way of life. Rather than allow the nation to be split and substantially weakened, a great Civil War was fought, which was extremely costly both in terms of lives and resources, but the nation was saved and the seeds of a superpower were sown. There are many who feel that our country is in as much danger of self-destruction today as we were prior to the Civil War because of the marked philosophical differences that divide us. During the Civil War, the issue at stake was slavery, whereas today the issue is personal responsibility versus governmental responsibility. Hopefully we will not have to engage in a political civil war before we achieve the kind of unity that will again bring us strength and prosperity.

There is perhaps more hope for our country than currently meets the eye. It would seem as if we are hopelessly gridlocked by Democrats and Republicans, each with very different ideas of government and its role in our lives. The ray of hope is found in the fact that there is an ever-increasing number of Independent voters who sometimes vote one way and other times vote another way, and therefore cannot be taken for granted by either party. There is also the rise of the Tea Party, which is interested in limited government according to the United States Constitution, capitalism with free enterprise, tax reform, sovereignty of the states consistent with the Constitution, border control, and fiscal responsibility. The very fact that so many people are joining the Tea Party or becoming politically Independent suggests that people are less willing to be spoon-fed by a largely biased media and are thinking for themselves again.

I believe the new Tea Party is going to be very important in deciding the future direction of our country. By its very nature, it is unlikely to ever become a well-organized political party, and it represents different things to different people, but the one factor that brings all of its constituents together is the desire for individual freedom and less government in our lives.

NO BASIS FOR CLASS WARFARE

Having had the opportunity to experience virtually every economic class in our society firsthand, I have found very little difference between people from the lower-middle class all the way to the upper echelons of the upper class in terms of financial values and belief in a strong work ethic. Most of the rich in America do not expect special treatment, nor do they get it unless they pay handsomely for it. Our society is very egalitarian, with a kind of social mingling and camaraderie not found in other nations around the world.

I mention these values because there is really no natural basis for class warfare here in America. After all, relatively few people begrudge the wealthy of the things they have acquired honestly. *Honestly* is, of course, the key word there, for I also know few people of *any* socioeconomic status who are not outraged that so many Wall Street fat cats experienced personal financial windfalls during the financial meltdown of many financial institutions in 2008 and 2009.

There continues to be an element, primarily in the Democratic Party, however, who use such abuses of the capitalist system to constantly evoke class warfare. They know that if they can get poor people to believe that they are the ones advocating for them, and that the other party advocates only for the rich, then it is very likely that the poor will vote for them in overwhelming numbers—and, of course, there are a lot more poor people than there are rich people. By attempting to associate Americans who are well off due to their extremely hard work and honest efforts with those despicable, greedy financiers, they distort reality. For these are by no means the same kinds of people, and, in fact, the hard-working, honest rich are the primary providers of jobs that allow us to have a middle class in this country. If we demonize, persecute, and overtax such people, they will become unsure of themselves and considerably less productive, which will have a devastating impact on the general economy, both because they are not spending and because they are not creating jobs.

Class warfare is an artificial division created for political advantage, and it should be rejected outright by the American people—for we have far too many real problems to devote energy to artificial ones.

DO UNIONS TRULY UNITE OR DIVIDE?

Another growing division in our nation exists between people who are unionized and those who are not. The concept of unions is actually quite good, and they played a very important role in the industrial development of our nation. The initial idea was "strength through unity" to keep unscrupulous owners/employers from taking advantage of defenseless workers. Without them, it is unlikely that we would have ever developed a robust middle class.

As time has gone on, however, many employees who are already well protected, such as government workers, have insisted on unionizing in order to strengthen their hands during collective bargaining. Initially, this was about getting the highest possible salaries, but now collective bargaining includes tenure, vacations, class size for teachers, meals, and a host of other things that frequently are not available to the general public.

In many cases, unions have now evolved to gain unfair political advantage based on the numbers of potential votes that can be delivered and the amount of money that can be donated to political causes. Leaders of many of these unions see nothing wrong with coercing members to donate a portion of their salary for dues, which they use to create very large monetary war chests for political campaigns. They then elect politicians who are obligated to them, allowing them to further enhance their positions financially, socially, and politically. In a twist of history from unions' original intention, sometimes the *unions* become the bullies against whom other people need protection. I do not believe that the average union worker grew up thinking that they should have unfair advantages over everyone else, but many union leaders try to create an entitlement mentality among their constituents. Once people get used to having certain advantages, they will fight vigorously to keep them.

Again, it is time for us as a nation to step back and ask ourselves, who is really being treated unfairly—unionized government workers or taxpayers who have to support unaffordable benefits? If we can just stop being selfish and think about "liberty and justice for all," we will not tolerate rabble-rousers endeavoring to create a need and a well-paid position for themselves.

Having said all of that, there are businesses and industries that do try to take advantage of individual workers, and unions are very effective in those situations—but this does not mean that everyone needs a union. If physicians were unionized, it is likely that they would bargain for higher pay and fewer hours. It is unlikely that they would accept the sometimes meager reimbursements from insurance companies, and they would demand significant tort reform. I can hear the union bosses saying that those are just the things that doctors should be complaining about, and that they are foolish to allow themselves to be abused by an unfair system. I fully agree that many aspects of the medical profession are less than optimal, but we have jobs that allow us to help people and save their lives. These jobs provide a great deal of fulfillment and satisfaction, and there is no need to squeeze every drop of blood out of the proverbial turnip. If physicians join together, however, and demand job perks for us as physicians simply because we provide a unique, indispensable service, doesn't that make us blackmailers? I am only using physicians as the example here because I am a physician, but the point is that it is rarely necessary to divide ourselves into special interest groups to gain advantages, and that much more progress can and will be made when we place our emphasis on creating opportunities for *everyone* as opposed to creating unfair advantages for those with the power to do so.

Progress in the Race Against Racism

The election of Barack Obama as the first black president in 2008 was a momentous occasion and signaled the fact that race was no longer a barrier to election to the highest office in the land. However, people still disagree about whether or not the United States remains racially divided.

Over the last two decades, I believe a great deal of progress has been made. During that time, many minorities have assumed important and very visible positions in our society and performed extremely well, eliminating anxiety on the part of the majority about their capabilities. Today one would have to live a fairly sheltered life in a highly biased community to harbor the belief that someone is inferior simply because of the color of their skin.

This does not mean that racism has disappeared completely from America, but it is gradually becoming a dinosaur in communities of educated people. I do know some who feel quite differently and think racism is alive and well. When I was a psychology major in college, one of the things I learned—which in retrospect is really only common sense—is that people tend to see what they are looking for. If you think someone likes you, you are likely to interpret their words and actions very differently than if you think they hate you. Prejudice is generally born out of ignorance and the propagation of myths; fortunately, Hollywood and the media have eliminated a great deal of misinformation about different races and nationalities.

In the national elections of 2012, we will have a wonderful opportunity to really see whether we have largely vanquished racism in America. Part of that final shift will require white America to set behind them the notion that most black candidates running for office share the same political left-wing leanings held by President Obama, and to embrace the process of scrutinizing candidates' positions rather than simply making assumptions about them. Doing so will help confirm that the evil of racism is losing its hold in this nation once defined by it.

DO OUR RELIGIOUS BELIEFS DIVIDE?

Unlike the division caused by racism, which seems to be shrinking, the division caused by religious differences seems to be intensifying, with the greatest conflict between Islam and Christianity. I was recently at a university-hosted dinner for a well-known expert on Islamic culture, and I asked him if it were possible for Islam and Christianity to peacefully coexist. It was clear that the question made him very uncomfortable, but he answered it honestly and said, unfortunately, it is not possible because some Islamists believe that Christians and Jews are infidels who should either be converted or at the very least avoided. It is very important to remember, however, that there are 1.4 billion Muslims in the world and to paint them with a single philosophical brush is just as absurd as trying to characterize the diverse thinking of billions of Christians around the world.

Perhaps the real problem with Islam is its radical faction, which has grown dramatically in recent years. Large groups of Muslim youths growing up in poverty-stricken areas in the Middle East and Africa, without a great deal of exposure to other religions and cultures, become relatively easy pickings for radical Islamic terrorists. These terrorist factions extract portions of the Koran, which they distort and use to convince these energetic but misdirected young people to join the "holy jihad" and receive an everlasting reward. With more than one billion Muslims in the world, there are certainly enough radical Islamists among them to cause concern. It is the quickest expanding religion in the world, but by births not by conversions. With a number of that magnitude and the intensity of their hatred, it is easy to see how this can be an enormous problem both now and in the future. At least knowing the numbers gives us some perspective on whether this problem can be ignored or deserves our full attention and efforts to address it.

Christianity, Islam, and Judaism all sprang from the seed of Abraham, which might lead one to believe that the religions should have enough in common to peacefully coexist. And if you exclude the radical elements of each religion, harmony should be within reach since peace, love, and fairness are foundational pillars of each of the religions. Since the vast majority of each religion's constituents embrace the concept of peace, it is incumbent upon those members to control their radical elements. This means they have to confront the radical elements who advocate violence and often the very principles that constitute their belief system. This must be done both publicly and privately, and they have to use every means available to them to eliminate this cancer among them. If they are afraid or refuse to stand up to the radicals among them, they will share in the guilt for the worldwide holocaust that will ensue. The only way in which religious division will not be highly destructive is if people embrace and live up to the precepts and principles of their respective religions.

WHAT THEN UNITES US?

In conclusion, many other factors such as sexism and ageism threaten our unity as a nation, but perhaps the most important factor is not what divides us, but rather what unites us.

Proverbs 29:18 says, "Where there is no vision, the people perish." One defining feature of an outstanding leader is the ability to bring divergent groups together and unite them in a common mission with benefits for all. Unfortunately, it is becoming increasingly difficult to discern what the vision for America is. Do we really know who we are and what we stand for? Do we know what we believe in, or are we constantly walking around with our fingertips in the air, trying to decide which way the wind is blowing at any given moment? Are we willing to think for ourselves, or do we believe media pundits have all the answers? Our founding fathers placed so much emphasis on nurturing a well-educated populace because they knew that our system of democracy could not long survive with ignorant and uncaring citizens who could easily be manipulated by slick politicians.

As we enter the next election season, I hope we will each be willing to take a step back and ask the question, what is of crucial importance to me and to the future of our nation?

—Chapter 12—

Liberty and Justice for All

Growing up changes one's definition of what is fun — maturation does that, thankfully — so I hate to admit now that as a boy I thoroughly enjoyed throwing rocks at cars. It was a thrill to wait in hiding, ambush the car driving by, and then make our escape. Occasionally, a driver would stop their vehicle and get out to yell at us. But if we were really fortunate, they would chase us. We would run just far enough ahead to encourage them, but when they got close, we would turn on the afterburners of youth, leaving them far behind while we laughed hysterically.

Once in a while, the police would come by — usually in unmarked cars — and the chase would be much more dramatic until we reached the ten-foot-tall fences at the end of the neighborhood field. To the police, it must have appeared as if they had us trapped. They had no idea, however, how practiced we were at vaulting those fences. We treated it like an Olympic event, running at full speed toward the fence and then leaping high into the air, grabbing the chain links, and allowing the momentum of our feet to swing us over the top and down on the other side. We would laugh at the police as we ran off, knowing there was no way they would follow us.

Today I have great admiration for the police, who risk their lives on a daily basis to protect *our* lives, freedom, and property. Remove all police protection in our society for just a day, and imagine the mayhem that would ensue. Sure, corruption exists in some police departments, because police officers are human beings like the rest of us; give power to human beings and corruption naturally follows. But police provide far greater good than bad in our society. Our justice system may have plenty of opportunities to malfunction, but we should not give up on it and must continually, objectively evaluate potential improvements.

When I started reading as a boy and began getting serious about my future, I was deeply encouraged by stories of those who had gone from rags to riches. One of the things virtually all of them had in common was that they benefitted from the freedom and justice in our system of government. I believe that all of these people would tell you that the only thing they really ever asked for was a fair chance to work hard, prove their worth, and benefit personally from their own efforts.

When we stand, place our hand over our heart, and before our country's flag pledge "with liberty and justice for all," we are simply saying that we want a nation that allows everyone to pursue their dreams as long as they are not injuring someone else, and that we will protect their right to do so. We should never underestimate the huge role that our justice system carries out in creating "fair play," allowing individuals to be successful in a large and complex society where given half a chance bullies will take advantage of anyone. Our legal system is rather large and cumbersome, but in the long run I would not trade it for any other system in the world.

I was recently summoned to fulfill my civic duty as a petit juror. When I first received the notice, I began thinking of all the patient surgeries and clinical appointments I would have to cancel in order to serve, but then I remembered that an obligation is an obligation no matter who you are and what you have to do. If some of us think we are too important to fulfill our civic duties, the very strength that our wonderful judicial system is built on in drawing from a diverse pool of jurors breaks down. I will confess that I was in the courthouse from 8:30 a.m. until a little after 6 p.m. essentially wasting my time. I was being considered as a juror for two cases, both of which were medical malpractice cases, and I knew there was no way on earth that the plaintiff's attorneys in either case would accept a neurosurgeon as a juror. I'm sure the judges knew that also; nevertheless, we spent several hours going through the motions and eventually jurors were selected. Do I think there are more efficient ways to select jurors? Of course I do. But I also realize that there will always be imperfections and room for improvement, and as long as we continue to work toward those improvements without being overly critical, we will make progress on improving a system that is already one of the best in the world.

My first time in court — and one of the only times — I was a neurosurgical resident at Johns Hopkins. I had been driving my car on a newly opened stretch of highway, going fifty-five miles per hour, when I was pulled over by a policeman.

"Sir, did you know that you were exceeding the speed limit by fifteen miles per hour?" he asked.

I was still surprised and confused about why I had been pulled over. "Well," I replied, "I was only going fifty-five. The speed limit is fifty-five miles per hour."

"No, sir," he replied. "The speed limit here is forty miles per hour."

"Where is that posted?" I asked.

"At the entrance to the highway, sir." He issued me a speeding violation and told me that I should go to court if I felt strongly about it.

Ultimately, I did decide to go to court to plead my case, but when I arrived and was waiting for my turn to approach the bench, I began having second thoughts about the wisdom of being there as I watched how stern the judge was with others. Finally it was my turn and I approached the bench.

"What do you do for work?" asked the judge.

"I am a neurosurgical resident at Johns Hopkins Hospital," I replied.

He looked up. My answer had brought a smile to his face. "Do you happen to know a neurosurgeon there by the name of Dr. John Chambers?"

"Sure," I said. "I operate with Dr. Chambers all the time."

"He's a good fishing buddy of mine," the judge said thoughtfully. He paused a moment. "Case dismissed," he said. "Next case." The poor police officer who had given me the ticket was astonished, and I exited the courtroom triumphantly.

Although it may seem that the judge was unfairly biased in my favor, I'm sure he knew the facts of the case and also knew that I had a perfectly clean driving record. Nevertheless, this case does point out how arbitrary some decisions can be—and those decisions can have profound effects on people's lives. This is the reason the founders of our judicial system inserted a provision to recall or dismiss rogue judges. They realized that judges are also people who can be quite imperfect like the rest of us, or who can become corrupted or even demented.

I do not wish to imply that our nation is the only nation with a solid judicial system. After I finished my neurosurgical residency at Johns Hopkins, Candy and I spent a year in Australia—as I mentioned earlier—where Murray, our oldest son was born. One evening we were driving down a hill and noticed a large number of cars at the bottom, some of which were police cars. We were soon stopped by a police officer on the street, who stated that we were exceeding the speed limit. The police had set up a speed trap at the base of the hill, realizing that almost everyone would be speeding by the time they hit the bottom due to their momentum. They were using radar guns, which they were all too happy to show to the disgruntled, entrapped travelers. I argued with the police, stating that they were engaging in entrapment. I told them that I was an American citizen and that we rarely did such things in America. They invited me to go to court and state my case, which I decided to do.

The judge there must have been in a particularly bad mood because he was slamming everyone, most of whom had legal counsel. Alone in a foreign country, I was feeling very vulnerable, and I asked God to give me wisdom as I approached the bench. The judge had already heard about the circumstances of my case, because some of the other victims of that evening had just argued in vain for mercy. I started my defense by talking about radar equipment and their use of Doppler waves to detect speed. I told him that the accuracy of such equipment could legitimately be called into question when it is used on an angle, which rapidly degrades the accuracy of the detected waves. He was fascinated as I explained in detail some basic principles of physics. At the end of my discourse, he said, "Case dismissed."

Both the American judicial system and the Australian judicial system are based on the English system, which has long been recognized for its fairness. Integral to a fair justice system is the opportunity for the accused to present their case to an impartial judge or jury, with an opportunity to appeal the judgment. Because there are a limited number of courts and personnel, our judicial system can be somewhat cumbersome and time consuming, but it generally works.

How Many Lawyers Does It Take to ...?

As a neurosurgeon, I have had many opportunities to participate in courtroom proceedings involving medical malpractice claims. Fortunately, all of these appearances so far have been as an expert witness—primarily for the defendants—but in a few egregious cases, for the plaintiffs. Much of our time during these trials is spent trying to educate the jury about things most of them have very little knowledge about. Unfortunately, in many such cases, the outcome of the trial depends more on who establishes the best rapport with the jury and puts on the best dog and pony show rather than who has the facts on their side.

I simply do not have time to be an expert witness anymore, but two decades ago I served as one for a local neurosurgeon who had experienced a bad outcome with a spinal cord tumor. The defense attorneys warned me that the plaintiff had hired Dr. Harvey Wachsman as their chief attorney, and that he was very tough on opposing expert witnesses. Not only was he trained as an attorney, he had also trained as a neurosurgeon and he was president of the American Board of Professional Liability Attorneys. I was familiar with his name because he had done some presentations at national meetings of neurosurgeons on how to avoid getting to know people like him in court. I must admit he was quite an imposing figure, exuding an air of confidence. As an expert witness, I try to be very cooperative, accommodating, and pleasant to the opposing attorneys, while gradually moving them into a position where I can expose the folly of their argument before the jury. It turns out that Dr. Wachsman used much the same approach initially with his witnesses. There I was trying to lead him into a certain position, which would allow me to spring the trap, and he was doing the exact same thing to me. We quickly recognized what each other was doing, and we were having a fabulous time with our chess match.

After the case was over, we were talking in the hallway and discovered that we had many common interests, as well as children who were similar in age. That was the beginning of a long and close friendship and many interesting discussions about medical malpractice. One of the things I admire about Dr. Wachsman and about my own personal attorney, Roger Bennett, is that they would never accept a case that was without merit, even if they thought it could be settled, resulting in a nice fee for themselves. If all plaintiff's attorneys behaved in that manner, our judicial system would be much less congested, our society would be much less litigious, and the court's time would be utilized more efficiently, preventing another level of waste. Unfortunately, we have an overabundance of lawyers—all of whom need to make a living—and so we can expect to have excessive litigation in our society for a long time to come. I hope at some point the legal establishment will recognize the problem and attempt to regulate the number of attorneys produced. If they do not, society at large will have to produce a solution.

The English system does not have the same kind of problem with excessive litigation because they have a "loser pay" arrangement. In that system, if you bring a lawsuit against someone and you lose, you have to pay all court costs and fees associated with the lawsuit—on both sides. In our system, most medical malpractice lawsuits are engaged on a contingency basis, which means the plaintiff has no out-of-pocket expenses, even if the case is lost. It's basically like playing the lottery; you have very little to lose, and you might become a millionaire if you instigate a medical malpractice lawsuit. Whether we add a "loser pay" arrangement to our legal system or devise another solution, the plaintiffs should have some skin in the game. To be able to bring lawsuits against people with no risk to yourself is antithetical to a harmonious and fair society. Unjustly accusing someone is also libel, but by the time a countersuit against the initiator of the first lawsuit is complete, the damage has already been done to the medical practitioner, who has lost their reputation whether they are ultimately proved innocent or not.

Another consequence of having too many lawyers and administrative personnel is the proliferation of red tape and regulations surrounding almost everything in our lives. Lawyers and administrators are not bad people, but they tend to regulate things because that's what they're trained to do. If you have too many lawyers, overregulation naturally follows. Over the years, I have had an opportunity to deal with many personnel issues at the hospital, in the corporate world, and in the nonprofit world. I have observed how difficult it is to get rid of someone who is not performing their job well because employers fear a lawsuit for unjust termination. You will have to look far and wide to find someone who is more patient and understanding than I am when it comes to giving people a chance to prove themselves, but incompetence and lack of ethical behavior clearly exists in our society, and when allowed to go unchecked, the morale of others is damaged and the result is inefficiency, and in some cases, even a danger to others.

Are there some commonsense approaches to dealing with things such as unfortunate medical outcomes or job termination? Some will be quick to dismiss this question, saying that without protective regulations and threats of lawsuits, discrimination and bias by employers would reign supreme in the workplaces of America. This, of course, assumes that we have not matured at all from the days of segregation and Jim Crowism, which is a huge and probably inappropriate assumption. One must also bear in mind that media scrutiny and bad publicity are huge deterrents of abusive behavior today compared to decades ago. If we continue to sue and regulate for every possibility, however, soon the level of distrust and suspicion throughout our society will begin to provide a real challenge to healthy interpersonal relationships. I believe it is possible to change the atmosphere of antagonism to one that is friendly and oriented toward the resolution of problems if we can find a way to make litigation the last solution rather than the first.

WHO CONTROLS THOSE WHO CONTROL US?

A great deal of bureaucracy has been added to our government in order to control corruption, but what about corruption *in* the government—how do we control that? I am aware of numerous patriotic, humanitarian Americans who have been severely abused by components of our justice system, including one of my closest friends.

His parents immigrated to America from Italy and were extremely hard-working, salt-of-the-earth-type people. During the race riots in the late 1960s, their pizza shop was actually protected by rioters when everything else was being looted or burned, because of the respect with which they were held in the community.

He was trained as an oral surgeon and had a thriving practice, but in 1992 he bought a building for $275,000, renovated it, and six months later it was valued at $1 million. Realizing his talent for real estate development, he quickly became one of the most successful developers in his state and went on to complete successful projects in several other states.

My friend has the most wonderful family with a loving and caring wife and extremely bright children, all of whom have stellar academic credentials and not the slightest hint of being spoiled rich kids. In fact, all of their children have been heavily involved in programs to assist poor families. Our families have vacationed together for years, including spending Christmas together. We have such similar values and principles that our bonding was natural.

As his real estate business increased, the available time he had for practicing oral surgery decreased, and he sold his practice to a colleague. Unfortunately, that colleague was later accused of Medicare fraud, but he did not have deep pockets — so the investigating agents came after my friend, even though he no longer owned the practice. They meticulously examined fifteen years of his practice records for evidence of fraud and were only able to uncover two questionable bills, amounting to a total of $180. My friend owns a spectacular home, a Manhattan penthouse, two Ferraris, and a European villa. However, given the fortune he amassed, he lives modestly compared to the lifestyle he could have had if he so desired. I believe the lead agent was either jealous of his success or incorrectly concluded that he had organized crime connections that produced his wealth.

Even though they were unable to uncover any fraud in his record, he was told that they would take him to trial as a co-defendant with the buyer of the practice and would convince jurors that he had knowledge or turned a "blind eye" to the other doctor's activity. And that eventually he would end up in federal prison if he did not plead guilty to a federal offense in connection with the $180 discrepancy. Not wanting to put his family through so much trauma, he accepted their deal and was sentenced to a one-year house arrest and a $300,000 fine. I am convinced that the judge in the case knew my friend was innocent, and at sentencing made a point of saying "none" of his net worth and success in real estate had any connection to this case, and that he was confused. The result of all of this is that an outstanding American citizen who did everything by the book—who is one of the most ethical people I know and an extremely generous humanitarian—is now a felon who cannot vote. He is giving serious consideration to moving to another country.

I know of other examples of severe government abuses, but I don't want to give the impression that I think government is bad for us. We must, however, find a way to control excessive and inappropriate government intrusion into the lives of innocent, law-abiding citizens who currently have little or no defense against a bully that is supposed to protect us.

How Reasonable Are Our Freedoms?

Recently, the United States Department of Justice decided to defend a Muslim teacher in Chicago who had less than one year of seniority and wanted to take off three weeks in the middle of the school term to participate in a religious activity. She was denied the time off but decided to take it anyway and was consequently fired. The lawsuit alleged that the school violated her right to freedom of religion.

This is a complex case with many legal nuances, and I certainly believe that freedom of religion is one of the important founding principles of our nation. However, making reasonable accommodations for one's religious beliefs should be just that—reasonable! In this case, the religious requirement could have been satisfied at any time during one's life, which means the teacher could have worked long enough to accumulate adequate time off and could have arranged far in advance for adequate coverage of her absence during the school term. Again, this is simply applying common sense, which seems to be rapidly disappearing from our society. Far too often, instead of looking for reasoned, rational approaches to our problems, we play the race card or the religion card or some other card in an attempt to evoke an emotional response. Have we become a nation moved more by emotion than logic when it comes to our governance and legal judgments? In this case, by forcing the school system to accommodate this teacher's demand for special treatment to accommodate her religious beliefs, the Justice Department has created a slippery slope with no end to subsequent requests by others for special treatment.

This is an important case, because not only do the rights of the teacher have to be considered, but if one wishes to be fair, the rights of the children being taught and the rights of the school who planned on having a teacher for the entire school year have to be considered. I understand the attorney general's desire to make sure that the teacher's rights are not trampled, but if our government is to be successful, it cannot have a myopic view of cases with such profound ramifications.

That same myopic view by our Justice Department resulted in the dismissal of three of the defendants in a voter intimidation case against the new Black Panther party in Philadelphia. The case was widely publicized because the incident was captured on film and distributed on YouTube, showing them verbally abusing voters and brandishing weapons. Would the Justice Department recognize such activity as voter intimidation if the perpetrators wore white sheets and burned crosses? I have a feeling that we may find out the answer to that question sooner rather than later if we continue to tolerate legal myopia justified by emotionally based, politically correct prejudices.

I am not accusing anyone of anything other than failing to look at the big picture when dealing with important legal matters. Some will say that I am advocating a conservative approach to the two cases we just discussed, but I would strongly disagree and would say that this is neither a conservative nor liberal view, but rather a practical and logical one. If we can just tone down the rhetoric and discuss things like rational human beings, applying justice equally and not based on some political philosophy, we will validate that phrase at the end of our Pledge of Allegiance, which advocates "justice for all."

LIBERTY FOR ALL—AND PRIVACY FOR SOME

We could write an entire book on the concept of "liberty for all" found in our Pledge of Allegiance, but I will concentrate on one related problem that threatens to severely derail our entire system of government. We frequently hear the question, why do many of the brightest and most accomplished people in our society refuse to run for public office? The answer is simple; they do not enter political contests because they know that their lives will be scrutinized and privacy and consideration for their family will be nonexistent. If some unsavory incident from the person's past is uncovered—or even suspected in the case of someone that the biased media does not like—a feeding frenzy occurs.

I do not believe this was the result our forefathers envisioned when they fought so hard to establish freedom of the press. Such freedom should be coupled with common decency and not serve as a license to be obnoxious and inconsiderate of fellow citizens one disagrees with politically. I do not believe that the press should be restricted, but it would be very helpful if our leaders would provide consistent commentary about the role of the press in politics. It is quite immature to favor the press that agrees with a leader's political philosophies and shun the press that is critical of a leader's positions.

Everyone has made mistakes in the past that they would prefer to keep private. If criminal activity went unpunished or there is a character defect relevant to the public position being sought, full disclosure and discussion is warranted, but if—as in most cases—it is just a juicy tidbit, the media should resist the urge to exploit it and concentrate on issues relevant to the job. I personally would be skeptical of someone who had never made mistakes, because they would probably have difficulty identifying with the rest of us. I realize that I'm asking a lot of the media, who now have twenty-four-hour news cycles and have to find a way to fill the time. There are numerous positive and uplifting stories about incredible people in this nation and throughout the world that could easily fill the time and provide inspiration. By the same token, it is totally irresponsible for the media to ignore glaring warning signs from a candidate's past just because they agree with his political philosophy. We should certainly not be surprised, however, when our children are mean and unfair to one another if we continue to provide them with such examples of hostility toward those with whom we disagree.

SHOWING KINDNESS TO THE POOR

When it comes to liberty and justice for all, the Bible makes it clear that we have a responsibility to be kind to the poor among us. As the famous old Chinese proverb points out, it is better to teach a poor man how to fish than to give him a fish. America did not become a great nation by encouraging people to feel sorry for themselves and seek handouts from others.

If we really want to eradicate poverty, we should allocate significant resources and personnel toward providing education and opportunity for the poor. And if we are to provide assistance to our able-bodied citizens, it should be attached to a requirement for work or acquisition of education and/or skills. Not only will this improve self-esteem, it will prepare those individuals to participate in an increasingly sophisticated workforce. Work projects could also contribute to the maintenance of our national infrastructure and beautification, if the right kinds of jobs are assigned as a requirement for benefits.

If they have to work anyway, many people will put real effort into finding the kind of job they want as opposed to collecting unemployment benefits and being assigned to work they consider undesirable. Some conservatives would say that we should leave such people on their own to sink or swim because we cannot afford to keep supporting them, while some liberals would say that these people already have enough problems and that it would be unfair to require anything of them that would add to their stress. I reject both of those positions and simply say the application of logic once again will prove most helpful in the long run to our fellow citizens experiencing financial misfortune.

IN FAIRNESS TO ALL

Every citizen of the United States should be expected to contribute to its welfare, which requires a fair system of taxation. We currently do not have such a system, because our tax code is so complex that those with good tax attorneys or accountants can find numerous loopholes to avoid paying their fair share of taxes. For instance, one well-known celebrity owns a very expensive mansion on a large piece of property in the Northeast, but pays very little in the way of property taxes because he raises honey bees on the property, which provides a little-known but gigantic tax benefit. I could go on for hours with similar examples, but the point is that given our country's financial crisis, the creation of a new and fairer tax system is urgently needed. The cries of "tax the rich" in the face of such a hypocritical tax code is, frankly, quite laughable. I do not believe that the rich are unpatriotic because they take advantage of loopholes, but I think we as a nation are smart enough to come up with a system of taxation that eliminates the need for slick accountants and lawyers, and that allows everyone to contribute proportionately to the financial health of the nation—just as God designed for us in the concept of the tithe.

Although I have pointed out many problems that we currently face as a nation, I have also made it clear that the principles upon which our government was founded are solid. In order to take advantage of the ingenious document known as the United States Constitution, we need outstanding, nonpartisan leadership with a vision that can unite the various political factions into a positive driving force, inspiring us and creating an atmosphere in which liberty and justice do flourish, allowing all to succeed.

CHAPTER 13

WHAT'S GOOD ABOUT AMERICA?

IT IS A TESTIMONY TO ALL that is good about America and the opportunities available here that a friend of mine was able to start out as a short order cook in a Kentucky Fried Chicken restaurant and, from there, through hard work and carefully observing the values that lead to success, established his own national chain of fast-food restaurants. As with any good rags-to-riches story, however, his life wasn't always easy.

Born to an unwed mother he never knew, he was adopted after six weeks. His adoptive mother died when he was five, and his father went in search of work around the country. From his family, my friend learned the value of hard work and perseverance, and in his early thirties, this young entrepreneur was given the opportunity to use his restaurant experience to take over four Kentucky Fried Chicken restaurants in need of help in Columbus, Ohio. He was able to completely turn around those restaurants, and four years later he sold them back to KFC, making approximately $1.5 million. That was just the beginning of his success, as he went on to found his own national fast-food chain.

"Only in America," he was once quoted as saying, "would a guy like me, from humble beginnings and without a high school diploma, become successful. America gave me a chance to live the life I want and work to make my dreams come true. We should never take our freedoms for granted, and we should seize every opportunity presented to us."[1]

His name of course is Dave Thomas, the founder of Wendy's, and my wife and I were among his first houseguests after he built his dream home in Fort Lauderdale prior to suffering a fatal heart attack. The effect that he has had on America has been overwhelmingly positive. Adopted himself, he went on to found the "Dave Thomas Foundation for Adoption." He claims his decision to drop out of high school was his biggest regret, and so not only did he go on to get his GED at around age sixty, he started the Dave Thomas Education Center to help other adults complete their GED.

Dave Thomas's success is not rare in our country because of the freedoms we enjoy, and like him and so many others, I am incredibly thankful to call America home. I have been privileged to travel the world and visit all of its major societies, but to be born in a land of opportunity for anyone willing to work hard is an unfathomable blessing that should never be taken for granted. As I learned growing up, even with all the economic turmoil that surrounds us today, entrepreneurial opportunities still exist for anyone who is willing to work hard and think innovatively.

The more stories I read about the success of people who applied themselves to make their lives better, the more motivated I am to be one of them. Knowledge really is power, and when I became a voracious reader, my confidence and grades improved accordingly. I needed little in the way of pep talks by adults, and today it is my strong belief that if you can just get children to believe in themselves and understand that when they achieve academically, they are the ultimate beneficiaries, they will do what is necessary to become a successful contributor rather than a drain on society.

God has opened many doors of opportunity throughout my lifetime, but I believe the greatest of those doors was allowing me to be born in the United States of America.

STEADY AS SHE GOES IN A SEA OF WORLDWIDE TROUBLE

Growing up, I heard many complaints from those around me about poverty, but visiting such places as India, Egypt, and Africa has provided me with perspective on what poverty really is. Hundreds of millions, if not billions, of people in the world live on less than two dollars a day. Many of those living in poverty in this country, in fact, would be considered quite wealthy by poor people in other countries. Also, here in the US, there is no caste system to determine one's social status, so there are many opportunities for people to escape poverty without resorting to a life of crime. You are much more likely to be judged in this nation by your knowledge and the way you express yourself than you are by your pedigree. I'm not sure we realize how good we have it on this point.

As I mentioned earlier in the book, racial identity has also become significantly less important in many segments of American society today, which is quite astonishing considering how strong racism was when I was a child. Considering the fact that prejudice is borne out of ignorance, I feel very optimistic about the future of race relations and diversity in America—something that in many countries around the world is worsening. This land was originally occupied by Native Americans, who were largely destroyed by European diseases to which they had no immunity. Hispanic populations then became the majority, followed by people of European ancestry. If you throw in the effects of slavery, East Indian and Asian immigration, and our lack of southern border controls today, you have a formula for perhaps the greatest human diversity on earth right here in the United States. That diversity, however, is a strength, because every group brings its own particular set of strengths to the table, and all have made very substantial contributions to the growth and development of our country. It is essential that we recognize these differences as the blessings they are.

When you look around the world—particularly at the Middle East right now—violent political turmoil is everywhere. Regime change in other parts of the world is often accompanied by bloodshed and severe upheaval. In 2008, our country experienced a radical political change of direction without firing a single bullet or taking a single prisoner. The ability to make such monumental changes without civil war is a mighty testament not only to our founders, but also to our current political leaders in all parties. If, in the future, our political leaders begin advocating violence to get their way, we should abandon them in droves and do everything possible to diminish their influence. Our system of representative government allows the people to periodically dismiss those elected officials who no longer represent their views. It is perhaps the most important civic duty of every citizen to inform themselves about the issues of the day and cast educated votes for people who truly represent their views. One should never vote for someone simply because they recognize their name or because of party designation. It is better to vote for no one at all than to cast an arbitrary vote. If all citizens take this duty seriously, there will be far less chance of our lifestyle and that of our children being hijacked by smooth-talking politicians.

FREEDOM TO MIND OUR OWN BUSINESS
Have you ever thought about how fortunate we are to have the right to privacy in such a technologically advanced society? Since 9/11 it has become increasingly important to monitor all suspicious activity in an attempt to prevent further terrorist attacks. One of the results of this monitoring has been the

discovery of some unsavory habits and characteristics of many otherwise out-standing citizens. To its credit, our government has not disclosed those find-ings or prosecuted the involved individuals because we still respect the right of all of our citizens to privacy as long as they are not infringing upon the rights of others. I realize that many "holier than thou" conservatives and even some liberals think we should use all gathered information about people they don't care for, to discredit them. If and when this begins to happen, our country will become a nightmare akin to George Orwell's novel *1984*. We must jeal-ously guard every American citizen's right to live as they please, again as long as they are not interfering with the rights of other Americans to do the same.

As a Bible-believing Christian, you might imagine that I would not be a proponent of gay marriage. I believe God loves homosexuals as much as he loves everyone, but if we can redefine marriage as between two men or two women or any other way based on social pressures as opposed to between a man and a woman, we will continue to redefine it in any way that we wish, which is a slippery slope with a disastrous ending, as witnessed in the dramatic fall of the Roman Empire. I don't believe this to be a political view, but rather a logical and reasoned view with long-term benefits to family structure and the propaga-tion of humankind. When children grow up in an environment with loving parents who provide security, they are free to be happy and playful and eager to learn. God obviously knew what he was doing when he ordained the traditional family, and we should not denigrate it in order to uplift some alternative.

However, I have no problem whatsoever with allowing gay people to live as they please, as long as they don't try to impose their lifestyle on everyone else. Marriage is a very sacred institution and should not be degraded by allowing every other type of relationship to be made equivalent to it. If gays or non-gays wish to have some type of legal binding relationship that helps with the adjudication of property rights and other legal matters, I certainly have no problem with that, but to equate that with marriage is going further than necessary. Likewise, I have no problem with Muslims or other religious groups who want to practice their religion in their homes, which may be vastly different from traditional Judeo-Christian religion, as long as they don't try to impose that on others or violate our laws. I could go on with other examples for quite some time, but I hope I have conveyed the wonderful free-dom we enjoy as citizens of a government that protects the right to privacy.

I was recently watching a National Geographic special about baboons, and one of the things that shocked me was the fact that dominant female baboons who lose their babies often forcibly abduct the babies of subordinate females. Unfortunately, in many societies around the world, the strong prey upon the weak like this. I am not naïve enough to believe that the same thing would not happen in our country if our police and military, backed by a moral government, were not available at a moment's notice to stop such barbarous activity. We take for granted our ability to accumulate material goods and have them protected by the government, but this is by no means a universal right.

I have lived the vast majority of my life in the state of Maryland, but it is a wonderful feeling to know that I can move to Texas next week or Alaska or Hawaii or anyplace else I decide to live. Not only can I choose in which state I want to reside, but I don't have to learn a new language or new customs. There are many parts of the world where chronic unemployment is the rule rather than the exception, and if I am unemployed and a new factory with thousands of job openings is announced in Idaho, I can quickly move there to take advantage of that opportunity. This means that if my priority is having a job rather than enjoying a location, I can almost always have a job. In my lifetime, I have held numerous jobs, from high school and college laboratory assistant to bank teller, to mailroom clerk, to assembly line worker, to radiology technician, to encyclopedia salesman, to student policeman, to Hollywood extra. Through all of these jobs, I have acquired knowledge and different skills, which are all very helpful to me today. In many societies, a person is pigeonholed into a single track, and basically has to spend their entire life working in that particular area. Here in the United States, however, we can go anywhere we want, take any job offered to us, and pursue the occupation of our choosing.

I also feel blessed to live in a country where I can openly choose and express my faith without fear of persecution. There are several places in the world today where conversion to Christianity will result in persecution or even execution. It is very sad that civilization has not advanced in some parts of the world to the point of being able to tolerate different ideas. In this country, we must guard against a tendency to require monolithic thought as imposed by political correctness. This is an insidious evil that robs people of their God-given desire to think for themselves. It is tyrannical and cruel, not even sparing young children in school. We must never forget that our nation was founded by people trying to escape religious intolerance and tyranny. Whenever we see these monsters raising their heads we should quickly slay them again.

OUR NATION'S CUP RUNS OVER

When disasters occur in other countries, who is first on the scene with massive aid? The United States, of course. It does not matter whether the mishap befalls a friend or an enemy, we are always there. It doesn't matter whether it's a very poor country such as Haiti or a very rich country such as Japan, we are still always there. Our compassion for and aid to other countries is unprecedented in the history of the world. Our compassion extends not only to food and material help during natural disasters, but during the recent Libyan civil war, we joined a multinational effort to prevent mass slaughter of the insurgents. Whether we can continue to be so generous in face of massive budgetary deficits remains to be seen, but we can certainly take pride in the historical humanitarian efforts of our nation.

When I was eight years old, I told my mother that I wanted to be a doctor.

"Benny," she said, "you can be anything in this world you want to be."

Although it was an arduous road filled with obstacles and grueling hours, I was able to realize my dream because of the generous freedoms we enjoy here in our nation. It is this ability of anyone to achieve their dreams that is perhaps the greatest thing about America.

There are few places in the world where people enjoy the level of freedom we have in America. Here you don't have to ask anyone's permission to start a new career or move to a new location. You are free to associate with whomever you please, and you are free to speak your mind if you decide not to allow yourself to be constrained by political correctness. If you have a fabulous idea, you are free to put as much time and effort into it as you like, and if that idea results in a financial windfall, you are entitled to spend your money to your heart's desire—after you have paid your taxes, of course. You can worship however you choose without fear of persecution. Even the poorest people in our society live like kings compared to billions of desperately poor people throughout the world.

Why do we enjoy all of these and many more blessings? It is largely because we have a representative government that respects the rights of its citizens and protects the life and property of its citizens, and because we have a military powerful enough to defend us against intruders. It is because we have a free market economy that, when unfettered, acts as an economic engine more powerful than any the world has ever seen. Most importantly, we have a nation of faith so bold that we are willing to proclaim "In God We Trust" on every coin in our pockets and every bill in our wallets. We have enjoyed the blessings of the Almighty from the time when he aided a fledgling group of militiamen in defeating the most powerful empire on earth up until the present, as he protects us from unimaginable terrorist threats. There never has been and probably never will be again another place like America the Beautiful.

—CHAPTER 14—

WHAT DO WE BELIEVE AND IN WHOM DO WE TRUST?

A SUCCESSFUL YOUNG BUSINESSMAN loved to buy exotic gifts for his mother on Mother's Day, but he was running out of ideas one year when he encountered some amazing birds with the ability to dance, sing, and talk. He was so happy that he purchased two of them and couldn't wait to ship them off to his mother. On Mother's Day, he called her excitedly and asked, "Mother, what did you think of those birds?"

"Mmm," she answered, "they were good."

"Mother, you didn't eat those birds!" he said, unable to contain his shock. "Those birds cost five thousand dollars apiece. They could dance, they could sing, and they could talk!"

"Well," she calmly replied, "then they should've said something."

This funny story points out how important it is for us to speak up when confronted with danger. If we see our freedoms eroding around us and are afraid to stand up for what we value, we too will ultimately end up in the stew like those birds. Most Germans did not agree with Hitler's insane agenda, but their collective silence permitted an unimaginable human tragedy that stained world history known as the Holocaust. How might their nation's history and our world's history have played out differently if those who saw what was happening had taken a stand for what they believed?

When rights and freedoms are not exercised, they become meaningless. If America is to remain the land of the free and home of the brave, we must have the courage to say what we mean unequivocally. If we allow our speech to be stifled by the PC police, we will be unable to have honest conversations in the struggle to resolve political differences. The founders of this nation were well aware of what happens when free speech is stifled.

Of all the wonderful freedoms that characterize life here in America, freedom of speech is one of the most important. This was most dramatically demonstrated in a recent Supreme Court decision, which upheld the rights of members of the Westboro Baptist Church to display extremely offensive signs and shout obscenities during funeral services for veterans. They are an intolerant hate group that despises homosexuality and are angry with the military because gays are allowed to serve. There is almost no one who agrees with the Westboro Church, but because of the Supreme Court's decision to strictly interpret the Constitution, the rights of the church members could not be denied. Can you imagine how quickly this group would be executed in many other countries for doing such a thing, but ironically the very military they are criticizing provides them with the freedom to be so obnoxious.

I actually have some doubts about that legal decision, because the signs, obscenity, and noise infringe upon the rights of other Americans to assemble peacefully for the burial of one of their loved ones. If my right to free speech causes you actual harm, it becomes time to curtail my speech. (Obviously the preferable option would be for me to care enough about you not to hurt you by exercising my rights.) But interestingly, as a society we go to great lengths to protect the legal rights of fringe elements while at the same time imposing massive social restrictions on speech through political correctness. The real question is, will we as Americans, accustomed to freedom, continue to sheepishly submit to the purveyors of political correctness without recognizing its erosive effects on our freedom?

What each one of us says and does—and what our actions are collectively as a nation—is born out of what we believe. But if we never act on our beliefs, can we say that we truly value them? Can we say that we truly *believe*? And if we *do* believe enough to act, what is it that we as a nation feel passionately enough to sacrifice for? In other words, what is it that we stand for?

TRUE COLORS: OUR FLAG

A symbol points to a reality beyond itself—a wedding ring representing the circle of unending, unconditional love between a husband and wife, for example, or the Christian cross turning the ancient Roman instrument of humiliation and torture into a symbol for the abundant life found through the sacrificial death of Christ. Symbolism abounds when it comes to our United States government, but I'd like to look at three important ones, beginning with our flag.

Few things give me greater joy than watching color guards marching into an assembly with our country's distinctive flag held high. Everyone knows that there are thirteen stripes to represent the original thirteen colonies and fifty stars, each representing one of the fifty states. But what you may not know is that red represents hardness and valor. White represents purity and innocence. And blue represents perseverance, vigilance, and justice.[1] One of the largest American flags ever constructed was at the behest of General Armistead during the War of 1812. The British Royal Navy had launched a fierce bombardment on Baltimore's Fort McHenry, and they clearly had the upper hand. Their capture of Baltimore, which seemed imminent, would solidify a series of victories that had included massive destruction in Washington, DC, including the White House. The commander of the British fleet had sent word to the Americans at Fort McHenry that he did not want to utterly destroy them and that he would cease bombing them as soon as they lowered the American flag in surrender.

Francis Scott Key was an amateur poet on an official government mission approved by President James Madison to try to rescue some captives being held by the British. Key was being held on one of the British ships engaged in the battle since he had overheard some of the war strategy and the British did not want him to tip off the Americans. His heart was broken as he heard the British missiles streaming through the air, destroying one of the last American bastions of safety. There was so much smoke and debris from the fighting that he was unable to determine whether the flag was still flying until early the next day, when "by the dawn's early light" he witnessed the most beautiful sight he had ever seen: the torn and tattered stars and stripes of our flag, still proudly waving. Many historians feel that America's ability to repel that fierce attack was the turning point in the War of 1812, which eventually led to our triumph.

Every time I see our magnificent Stars and Stripes, I think of the fortitude of those Americans at Fort McHenry who, although outnumbered and outgunned, never allowed that flag to lower in surrender. That should remind us of who we are: a people who never surrender, who never give up, who are historically rooted in a faith in God rather than in the vicissitudes of man, who believe in freedom, and who would rather die than abandon our beliefs in equality and justice for everyone.

FLYING HIGH: THE EAGLE

Another of our proud symbols is the bald eagle. Some wanted a turkey as our national emblem, while others favored the golden eagle, but after much deliberation, the bald eagle was chosen because it symbolizes strength, courage, and freedom.

In *The 5000 Year Leap*, W. Cleon Skousen writes that the founders had many other symbolic reasons for choosing the eagle. But the reason that impressed me most is that in order for the eagle to fly straight, its two wings must be balanced. If either the left wing or the right wing is too heavy, the bird will veer off to one side and crash. The liberals represent the left wing and the conservatives represent the right wing. The liberals tend to have lots of great ideas that cost a great deal of money and, if left unchecked, would quickly bankrupt the nation. The conservatives simply want to maintain the status quo and are not very adventurous, and if our nation were left solely to their ideas, stagnation would occur. However, when you balance the right and left wings evenly, the eagle is able to fly high and straight, and the potential for progress is tremendous. Of course this is an oversimplification, and currently the conservative wing is putting forth some fairly bold ideas about how to maintain the fiscal responsibility of a nation, but ultimately that means they are trying to conserve the American dream for future generations.

As a nation, we need to understand that there are valid functions for people of all political persuasions. No party has a monopoly on truth and justice. What is called for is mutual respect and a willingness to make decisions based on facts and empirical data rather than philosophical tenets. If we can remember these things, then the majestic nature symbolized by the bald eagle will be a rightful representation of our wise nation.

OUR STATUE OF LIBERTY: WATCHING OVER THOSE YEARNING TO BREATHE FREE

When I was in high school, I determined to learn as much as I possibly could about everything. When I began studying European art and classical music, however, I received a significant amount of criticism from classmates. Some told me that those areas were not culturally relevant to me as an African-American. But if the United States of America is the diverse conglomeration of people from all kinds of cultural and ethnic backgrounds, what does the term *culturally relevant* mean to its citizens?

To answer that question, take a trip to Ellis Island, the resting place of our Statue of Liberty, which has become a widely recognized symbol of freedom and opportunity throughout the world. Walk through the museum where pictures of immigrants from every part of the world are displayed on the walls. Look at the determination in their eyes, many of whom brought to this country only what they could carry in their hands. These people were willing to work not just eight hours a day, but twelve, sixteen, or even twenty hours a day. They worked not five days a week, but six or even seven days to make their way in the "New World." At that time, there was no such thing as a minimum wage, but they didn't care. They were not working for themselves, but rather to provide an opportunity for their sons and daughters, grandsons and granddaughters, to prosper in this new land. It is the *hard work* of all those people from all those places that is culturally relevant to every American.

Long before the Statue of Liberty landed in America, however, other immigrants came here in the bottom of slave ships who worked even harder for no wages, but they too had a dream that one day their great-grandsons and great-granddaughters might pursue freedom and prosperity in this land.

Of all the nations in the world, the United States of America was the only one big enough and great enough to allow all those people from all those backgrounds to fulfill their dreams. It required the dreams and talents of all those people to create the quilt that is America. Every single one of us is culturally relevant to every other one of us—and that is why we are called the *United* States of America! Is the rapid rise of the United States really all that amazing considering the unprecedented freedom its citizens had? When citizens and, indeed, entire communities recognized that they would be the primary beneficiaries of their own hard work, there was no stopping them. It's like giving someone access to a vault full of money with two different scenarios. In the first instance, they are told that they can have the vast majority of the money that they are able to carry out over the next ten hours. In the second instance, they are told to work on behalf of the overseer who will make sure that they are treated fairly. Which scenario do you think will generate the greatest intensity of work? That's a no-brainer, of course, and until recent decades, it was a no-brainer that hard work and innovation here could vastly improve your personal circumstances and those of your family. This belief was and should continue to be a basic part of the American dream. If you truly believe this, you should resist any attempts to establish the government as your overseer rather than your facilitator. It was no accident that this philosophy accelerated the rise of America. If we abandon it—even by accident because we are sleeping—our fall will be just as rapid as was our rise.

IN WHOM DO WE TRUST?

Traditionally, America has been a God-fearing nation. Evidence of that can be found in our mottos, in many of our songs, in many of our national documents, and carved into many monuments and buildings.[2] It has traditionally distinguished us from many other nations of the world, and it is one of the reasons we are always first in line when it comes to humanitarian aid for others. It is also why we have not used our great might to conquer other nations of the world. We pay attention to the issues of morality and ethics because our nation was founded on principles revealed to us in the Bible by a righteous and just God.

Have you ever stopped to think about what money represents? It represents wealth and power. As we have recently seen, when you lack money and incur great debt, your influence and power decrease. Considering what your money says about you, it is really quite amazing that our nation has chosen to inscribe the phrase "In God We Trust" on all of our money. By doing so, we proclaim to the world that godly principles are essential to our way of life, that we trust not in our money, not in the power that comes from having money—but in our God. Having declared that for the world to see, it is essential that we allow our lives to speak as loudly as our money.

We have been favored by God because we have acknowledged him, but as the forces of political correctness attempt to push God out of our lives, we must have courage to resist them. That does not mean that we should retaliate or manifest the same intolerance they have shown. It does mean, however, that we must stand up and be counted. If they do not wish to accept the godly principles that we choose to live by, we should make no attempt to force them, but by no stretch of the imagination should we allow them to force their beliefs on us. For the God in whom we place our trust has entrusted each one of us with the freedom to choose our beliefs—as well as the mind to speak up for what we believe to be right.

COMPROMISE, OPINION, AND PRINCIPLES

The word *compromise* was referred to frequently during the debate in early 2011 about the national budget and again that summer in the debate about raising the debt ceiling. In general, compromise is good when dealing with issues about which there are legitimate differences of opinion. A problem arises, however, with the compromise of principles.

For example, if one believes that killing is wrong in all instances, be it executing a mass murderer or aborting an unborn fetus, it will be very difficult to negotiate a compromise on the issues of capital punishment or abortion.

If, on the other hand, an individual is opposed to capital punishment simply because of the great expense involved in each case, and only opposed to *late-term* abortion, that person would be quite capable of yielding to compromise.

As a nation, we need to spend more time understanding who we are and what those principles are that define us. Once we identify them, there should be no apology and no compromise in applying them. However, on less vital issues, it is important to recognize that we are all in the same boat and will reach our destination much faster if we row the boat together. Our elected leaders need to spend much more time understanding the values and principles that made us into a great nation, and much less time worrying about what their party platform has on its agenda. More importantly, the people who select the leaders must recognize that they ultimately are responsible for what is happening in the country. If they don't like it, they need to select different leaders. Each citizen should put at least as much effort into selecting their representatives as they do into buying a new car.

I live in a small town in rural Maryland, and I must say it is a very pleasant place to live. People still speak to those they don't know and are still willing to help someone in need. There was a time in America when people made a much greater effort to be neighborly. Now it is common for people to not even know their neighbors. People walk by others in their workplace who have been there for years and don't even acknowledge their presence. News commentators, political pundits, and public officials verbally savage those with whom they disagree and demonize their motives. This is all very sad to me because it seems that as time goes on, we should be becoming more civilized rather than less so. There is absolutely no moral justification for adults to spend valuable time disparaging their political opponents rather than delving into logical solutions for the problems that face us all. They, of course, justify it by their need to be re-elected. How can we blame children for bullying and trash talk when we provide them with such excellent examples of how to go about doing it?

I remember how much fun people in my high school had when they made fun of others. The people with the sharpest tongues were accorded the most honor and respect. It was only after I learned how to be verbally abusive to others that I was accepted as one of the guys in high school. But we were immature kids with poor judgment and lack of compassion; responsible adults can do much better, even though the temptation is always there to demonize those with whom we disagree.

During the civil rights movement, the media played a tremendous role in changing public perceptions and attitudes with regard to race. If they choose to do so, they could once again play an important role in rectifying the mean-spiritedness that threatens to destroy the harmony and progress of the world's most powerful nation. However, many people make a great deal of money by polarizing people and cultivating a following. It takes very strong character to resist the urge to denigrate others and create a wise and "all knowing" persona for themselves. I suspect that many in the media are pretty entrenched in their way of doing things and are not going to suddenly play fair. I should also point out that some in the media are real patriots and use humor, sarcasm, hyperbole, and satire in an attempt to awaken people to the realities of the times in which we live. Ultimately, the people still have the power, and just as they can rid themselves of undesirable politicians, they can vote with their money and remote controls, which will always have a powerful impact on the direction our media takes.

THE DIFFERENCE BETWEEN TOLERANCE AND ACCOMMODATION

Because of all the conflicting views necessitating compromise in our nation, the difference between tolerance and accommodation is an important one to understand. Principles of fairness and brotherhood should make us *tolerant* of everyone. We really do not have the right to *impose* our values and lifestyle on people who have a different point of view. For example, several years ago a fourth-year general surgery resident at a hospital in the Midwest tried to enlist my help because she was being fired for praying with patients before surgery. I asked her if the patients requested prayer and she said no, but she went on to state that they did not refuse to pray with her. I told her that she was abusing her position of power and that she needed to recognize her error and apologize to everyone involved. It is an abuse of power to make people pray just as it is an abuse of power to keep people from praying. Our founding fathers understood this and wisely instituted a policy of separation of church and state, which is totally different from the concept of separation of God and state.

I am happy that people with lifestyles with which I strongly disagree are free to live their lives as they please, as long as their lifestyle does not infringe upon my way of life. Some people, for example, believe in nudity as a way of life. I have no problem with them pursuing that belief in a nudist colony or some other place where young children would not accidentally be exposed to something they were not prepared for. That is *tolerance*. *Accommodation* might mean arming all the nudists with whistles, which they would be required to blow every time they rounded a corner in my community so that those not wishing to see them could turn their back or shelter their children.

This is of course an extreme example, but it clearly shows the difference between tolerance and accommodation. As God-fearing people, we should absolutely exercise tolerance, but changing our way of life to accommodate everyone is not only impractical, but it is also very unfair to the existing culture. Again, in order to be fair, we must have a firm grasp of who we are as a people and what is important to us. If we don't, the forces of political correctness will gradually blur the lines between tolerance and acceptance, to the point that we will soon have no idea who we are or what we stand for. This process has already begun in our nation, and we must recognize it in order to stop it in its tracks.

An example of how political correctness tries to usurp power and impose rules occurred a few years ago when some lawyers approached my wife and me to inform us that our "Think Big" banners could no longer be displayed in public schools. The letter T is for talent, which everyone has to some degree; the letter H is for honesty; I is for insight; N is for nice; K is for knowledge; B is for books; I is for in-depth learning; and G is for God. Because the G stands for God, they felt that was clearly a violation of the establishment clause of the First Amendment. We informed them that the First Amendment prohibits government suppression of religious expression and a rather vigorous argument ensued. I told them that we could resolve this at the level of the Supreme Court, which may have seemed like a bold and reckless statement. It really wasn't, because I knew that I was going to the Supreme Court the very next week to receive the Jefferson Award, and I figured I would ask Justice Sandra Day O'Connor while I was there. I did, and she said they had no idea what they were talking about, and that of course you could put such a banner in a public school without violating any part of the Constitution. The audacity of some of the secularists who try to get God out of everything with no legitimate legal backing is astonishing, and they must be challenged and their objections defeated if our value system is to survive.

BEING LOGICAL, NOT POLITICAL

By now you might have gotten the idea that I don't like people who practice political correctness, but that would not be true. Many such people think they are doing what is right and necessary to cultivate a civil society. I do, however, believe they are misguided. Instead of advocating for unanimity of speech and thought, they should be emphasizing learning to respect and be gracious to those with whom they disagree. Think about how boring the world would be if everybody agreed with everything you believed. As I love to say, "If two people believe the same thing about everything, one of them isn't necessary."

Many recent polls have shown that most Americans believe that we are on the wrong path as a nation. They are discouraged about our future and the future of our children. I say, be not discouraged, for God is on our side if we really trust in him, as is indicated on every coin in your pocket and every bill in your wallet.

We must stop being political and start being logical. The human brain has gigantic frontal lobes when compared with the brains of all other species. Why do we have these enlarged cerebral areas? The frontal lobes are where rational thought processing takes place, and it is there that information from the past and the present can be processed and integrated into a plan for the future. Unlike most animals, because we are so equipped, we do not have to simply react to our environment. We have the ability to plan and strategize, which allows us a great deal of control over our course in the future.

BUILDING ON OUR SOLID FOUNDATION

I feel blessed to have lived here in America for sixty years, with hopefully many more to come. In all those years, I have never met a perfect person — and since nations are simply collections of imperfect people, I have never seen a perfect nation. In looking back through the history of the world, however, I feel very comfortable in saying that there has never been another nation like the United States of America. Yes, we have made mistakes, but we continue to learn from them, and as long as we remain capable of embracing life, liberty, and the pursuit of happiness as our goal, and we are willing to guarantee those things to our citizens, I believe we will continue to grow in greatness.

When our forefathers knelt and prayed for wisdom at the Constitutional Convention in Philadelphia in 1787, then stood up and together assembled a seventeen-page document known as the Constitution of the United States of America, they were clearly guided by the hand of God. Today the forces of political correctness would expel God from every public sphere in American life, and the hearts and minds of every man, woman, and child in America are up for grabs in this cataclysmic battle between the lovers of men and the lovers of God. Some would rather never choose between the two, but life is full of choices, and our individual and collective choices determine the quality of our existence.

I believe it is time for us to stand up and be counted. We can no longer be passive because the Judeo-Christian way of life in America is at stake. We need not be ashamed of our faith, and we certainly should not allow those who believe differently to change who we are in order to be politically correct. Yes, we should accept them with brotherly love as we have been taught, but we should never compromise our belief system. We do believe in God, and we do believe in the right of everyone to have life, liberty, and the pursuit of happiness. We do believe in an orderly government that facilitates these goals rather than impedes them. It is time to set aside political correctness and replace it with the bold values and principles that founded our nation and caused it to race to the pinnacle of the world faster than any other nation in history. It is time to stop apologizing and to start leading, because the world is desperately in need of fair and ethical leadership. If that leader is not America, then who will it be, and where will they lead?

If we apply logic to solving our problems and add the godly principles of loving our fellow man, caring about our neighbors, and developing our God-given talents to the utmost so we become valuable to those around us — allowing these values and principles to govern our lives — then not only will we remain a pinnacle nation, we will truly be "one nation, under God, indivisible, with liberty and justice for all."

It is my prayer, America, that God will continue to shed his grace on thee, and crown thy good with brotherhood from sea to shining sea. I pray that with his blessings our past will be but a stepping stone to a bright future and that our best days will truly lie ahead of us — a beautiful new beginning!

Acknowledgments

I wish heartily to thank:

John Sloan, Sealy Yates, Bob Hudson, Bill Federer, Scott Macdonald, Don Gates, and the entire team who worked tirelessly to get this book published.

NOTES

CHAPTER 1: AMERICA'S HISTORY OF REBELLING FOR CHANGE

1. If you're an armchair historian thinking, *I have never heard of the Battle of Breed's Hill*, that's because in the confusion of battle some thought the skirmish took place at nearby Bunker Hill, but the actual fighting took place at Breed's. In fact, the Battle of Bunker Hill and the Battle of Breed's Hill are one and the same. Robert V. Remini, *A Short History of the United States* (New York: HarperCollins, 2008), 38.
2. Larry Schweikart and Michael Allen, *A Patriot's History of the United States* (New York: Penguin, 2004), 79.
3. Craig Nelson, *Thomas Paine: Enlightenment, Revolution, and the Birth of Modern Nations* (New York: Penguin, 2007), 90.

CHAPTER 2: WHO ARE "WE THE PEOPLE"?

1. See 2 Samuel 2:4, 1 Chronicles 29:22, 2 Chronicles 10:16, and Exodus 19:8.
2. Colin Rhys Lovell, *English Constitutional and Legal History* (New York: Oxford University Press, 1962), 3–50.
3. James MacGregor Burns, *The Vineyard of Liberty* (New York: Knopf, 1982), 33.
4. http://plato.stanford.edu/entries/aristotle-politics/ , section 3, chart under subhead "Supplement: Political Naturalism."
5. *Federalist Papers*, no. 10, 81.
6. *Federalist Papers*, no. 39, 241.
7. *Federalist Papers*, no. 51, February 8, 1788.

8. William J. Federer, *America's God and Country: Encyclopedia of Quotations* (St. Louis: Amerisearch, 2000), 458.

9. Federer, *America's God and Country*, 453.

10. Kenneth C. Davis, *Don't Know Much about History* (New York: HarperCollins, 2004), 118–19.

11. Letter to Colonel Edward Carrington (January 16, 1787); see www.wideworldofquotes.com/quotes/thomas-jefferson-quotes.html.

12. Letter to John Jay (August 15, 1786); see www.revolutionary-war-and-beyond.com/george-washington-quotes-9.html.

13. See www.spiegel.de/international/europe/0,1518,677214,00.html; www.marketoracle.co.uk/Article28957.html; http://economicsnewspaper.com/policy/german/portugal-ireland-belgium-italy-juncker-fears-contagion–35019.html; www.taipanpublishinggroup.com/tpg/taipan-daily/taipan-daily–062411.html?sub=TD&o=385937&s=389028&u=48412125&l=275791&g=198&r=Milo.

14. Matthew Spalding, ed., *The Founders' Almanac* (Washington, DC: Heritage Foundation, 2008), 203. Excerpted from a letter to Joseph Milligan, April 6, 1816.

15. *Notes on the State of Virginia*, Query XIV, 1781.

Chapter 3: Are We a Judeo-Christian Nation or Not?

1. Peter Lillback with Jerry Newcombe, *George Washington's Sacred Fire* (Bryn Mawr, Penn.: Providence Forum Press, 2006), 485–86.

2. Federer, *America's God and Country*, 635.

3. Federer, *America's God and Country*, 654. National Day of Thanksgiving Proclamation, October 3, 1789.

4. www.petahtikvah.com/Articles/salomon.htm.

5. www.jewishworldreview.com/jewish/salomon.asp.

6. nationaldayofprayer.org/about/history/.

7. www.christiannewswire.com/news/4387713640.html.

8. Federer, *America's God and Country*, 248–49.

9. Federer, *America's God and Country*: George Washington, 634; John Adams, 4; Alexander Hamilton, 273; Daniel Webster, 668; Thomas Paine, 489; John Locke, 397; John Madison, 409.

10. texaslegislativeupdate.wordpress.com/2011/05/18/liberty-institute-arguing-candy-cane-case-implications-for-first-amendment-rights-of–41-million-school-children-and-parents/.

11. www.proconstitution.com/under_god/.

CHAPTER 4: A DIFFERENT SCHOOL OF THOUGHT

1. www.npr.org/templates/story/story.php?storyId=11601692.
2. education.stateuniversity.com/pages/1878/Compulsory-School-Attendance.html, under subheading "Development of Compulsory School Attendance Philosophy and Laws," paragraph 3.
3. education.stateuniversity.com/pages/1878/Compulsory-School-Attendance.html, under subheading "Development of Compulsory School Attendance Philosophy and Laws," paragraph 7.
4. Education of slaves was forbidden in 1740. See www.campaignfor educationusa.org/us-public-education-timeline and www.pbs.org/wnet/slavery/experience/education/docs1.html.
5. Alexis de Tocqueville, *Democracy in America*. http://books.google.com/books, 337.
6. Federer, *America's God and Country*, 206 (source quote p. 746).
7. Federer, *America's God and Country*, 680.
8. Spalding, *The Founders' Almanac*, 150. Excerpted from a letter to WT Barry, dated August 4, 1822.
9. Ibid., 180. James Madison from *The Federalist Papers* number 10, November 23, 1787.

CHAPTER 5: CAPITALISM: ITS PROS AND CONS

1. www.inventions.org/culture/african/matzeliger.html.
2. www.horatioalger.com/index.cfm.
3. www.usatoday.com/life/people/obit/2010–03–30-stand-and-deliver-teacher_N.htm.
4. Matthew 25:14–30; Luke 19:12–28.
5. www.biblegateway.com/passage/?search=Matthew+25percent 3A14–30&version=NIV, "A talent was worth about twenty years' worth of a day laborer's wages."
6. www.encyclopediaofalabama.org/face/Article.jsp?id=h–2062.
7. Spalding, *The Founders' Almanac*, 158.
8. www.nytimes.com/2009/04/22/education/22dropout.html; www.msnbc.msn.com/id/23889321/ns/us_news-education/t/cities-cited-low-high-school-graduation-rates/; www.usatoday.com/news/education/2006–06–20-dropout-rates_x.htm; www.csmonitor.com/USA/Education/2010/0610/Graduation-rate-for-US-high-schoolers-falls-for-second-straight-year.

CHAPTER 6: SOCIALISM: WHOSE POT OF SOUP IS IT?

1. money.cnn.com/2011/04/19/news/economy/ceo_pay/index.htm.

2. Davis, *Don't Know Much about History*, 351.

3. freemasonry.bcy.ca/history/boston_tea_party.html, under subheading "December 16."

4. The following quotes can be found at http://conservativecolloquium .wordpress.com/2007/11/24/founding-fathers-on-charity-wealth -redistribution-and-federal-govt/.

"The democracy will cease to exist when you take away from those who are willing to work and give to those who would not."

"To compel a man to subsidize with his taxes the propagation of ideas which he disbelieves and abhors is sinful and tyrannical."

"A wise and frugal government ... shall restrain men from injuring one another, shall leave them otherwise free to regulate their own pursuits of industry and improvement, and shall not take from the mouth of labor the bread it has earned. This is the sum of good government."

Thomas Jefferson, First Inaugural Address, March 4, 1801

"To take from one, because it is thought his own industry and that of his fathers has acquired too much, in order to spare to others, who, or whose fathers, have not exercised equal industry and skill, is to violate arbitrarily the first principle of association, the guarantee to everyone the free exercise of his industry and the fruits acquired by it."

Thomas Jefferson, letter to Joseph Milligan, April 6, 1816

"God helps those who help themselves."

"The U.S. Constitution doesn't guarantee happiness, only the pursuit of it. You have to catch up with it yourself."

"There are two ways of being happy: We must either diminish our wants or augment our means — either may do — the result is the same and it is for each man to decide for himself and to do that which happens to be easier."

"He that waits upon fortune, is never sure of a dinner."

Benjamin Franklin

"It's not tyranny we desire; it's a just, limited, federal government."

"In the main it will be found that a power over a man's support (salary) is a power over his will." *Alexander Hamilton*

"The rights of persons, and the rights of property, are the objects, for the protection of which Government was instituted."

"The diversity in the faculties of men, from which the rights of property originate, is not less an insuperable obstacle to an uniformity of interests. The protection of these faculties is the first object of government. The class of citizens who provide at once their own food and their own raiment, may be viewed as the most truly independent and happy."

James Madison

"No power on earth has a right to take our property from us without our consent."

John Jay

"The moment the idea is admitted into society that property is not as sacred as the laws of God, and that there is not a force of law and public justice to protect it, anarchy and tyranny commence. If 'Thou shalt not covet' and 'Thou shalt not steal' were not commandments of Heaven, they must be made inviolable precepts in every society before it can be civilized or made free."

John Adams from A Defense of the
Constitutions of Government of the
United States of America, 1787

5. www.epi.org/publications/entry/briefingpapers_bp143/.
6. www.capitalresearch.org/pubs/pdf/v1246489837.pdf; http://www.thirdreport.com/third-report.asp?storyid=365; http://www.naked-capitalism.com/2009/04/socialism-gaining-ground-in-america.html; http://socialismdoesntwork.com/why-socialism-doesnt-work/; http://www.preservearticles.com/201102073940/merits-and-demerits-of-socialism.html.

CHAPTER 7: WHAT IS A MORAL NATION?

1. www.cic.gc.ca/english/work/index.asp.
2. Remini, *A Short History of the United States*, 274–81.
3. Ibid., 326–31.
4. Federer, *America's God and Country*, 240.
5. John R. Howe Jr., *The Changing Political Thought of John Adams* (Princeton, N.J.: Princeton University Press, 1966), 189.
6. ethicsalarms.com/2011/01/26/where-we-miss-morality-the-unmarried-mothers-disaster/; http://www.ocpathink.org/articles/354.
7. www.wftv.com/news/25813000/detail.html.

8. www.dailymarkets.com/economy/2010/07/21/the-total-us-debt-to-gdp-ratio-is-now-worse-than-in-the-great-depression/; http://useconomy.about.com/od/fiscalpolicy/p/US_Debt.htm; www.reuters.com/article/2010/06/08/usa-treasury-debt-id USN088462520100608.

9. For data on the United States's historical debt, see www.treasurydirect.gov/govt/reports/pd/histdebt/histdebt.htm.

10. freemencapitalist.com/founding-fathers/thomas-jefferson-biography/thomas-jefferson-quotes/, under subheading "Thomas Jefferson Quotes on Government Waste/Debt."

11. articles.cnn.com/2009 – 01 – 16/world/zimbawe.currency_1_zimbawe-dollar-south-african-rand-dollar-note?_s=PM:WORLD.

CHAPTER 8: LEARNING FROM OUR MISTAKES

1. See oxforddictionaries.com/definition/Motown). Motown: "The first black-owned record company in the US ... Motown was founded in Detroit in 1959 by Berry Gordy, and was important in popularizing soul music, producing artists such as the Supremes, Stevie Wonder, and Marvin Gaye." Motown was an "informal name for Detroit"; the term is "a shortening of *Motor Town*, by association with the car manufacturing industry of Detroit."

2. www.blackinventor.com/.

3. Albert Henry Smyth, ed., *The Writings of Benjamin Franklin* (New York: Macmillan, 1905 – 07), 3:135.

4. William V. Wells, *The Life and Public Services of Samuel Adams*, 3 vols. (Boston: Little, Brown and Company, 1865), 1:154.

5. www.working-minds.com/TJquotes.htm, {Issue #54}.

6. Ibid., {Issue #59}.

7. www.monticello.org/site/jefferson/democracy-will-cease-to-exist-quotation.

8. www.constitution.org/je/je4_cong_deb_12.htm.

9. Spalding, *The Founders' Almanac*, 188.

10. lifestrategies.thingseternal.com/topics/foundersoneducation.html; www.nccs.net/newsletter/apr99nl.html.

11. www.rutgers.edu/guides/glo-sov.html; www.heritage.org/Research/Lecture/Who-Lost-Russia; http://reasonovermight.blogspot.com/2005/06/cubas-decline-by-numbers.html; future.state.gov/when/timeline/1969_detente/fall_of_communism.html.

CHAPTER 9: AMERICA'S ROLE IN A WORLD AT WAR

1. library.uncg.edu/dp/wv/collection.aspx?col=887
2. www.history.navy.mil/photos/events/wwii-pac/pearlhbr/pearlhbr. htm, paragraph 5.

CHAPTER 10: IS HEALTH CARE A RIGHT?

1. Fifty-two million in 2010: www.bloomberg.com/news/2011–03–16/ americans-without-health-insurance-rose-to–52-million-on-job-loss-expense.html.
2. For more information, see Larry Schweikart, *The Entrepreneurial Adventure: A History of Business in the United States* (Ft. Worth, Tex.: Harcourt, 2000). See also www.american.com/archive/2009/ april–2009/Success-on-the-Side.

CHAPTER 13: WHAT'S GOOD ABOUT AMERICA?

1. From Dave Thomas's biography available on Wendys.com.

CHAPTER 14: WHAT DO WE BELIEVE AND IN WHOM DO WE TRUST?

1. www.ehow.com/about_4597645_do-colors-american-flag-stand.html; www.memorials.com/Flag-Cases-Flag-Color-Meaning-information. php.
2. www.allabouthistory.org/spiritual-heritage-and-government-monuments-faq.htm.

Gifted Hands

The Ben Carson Story

Ben Carson, M. D., with Cecil Murphey

In 1987, Dr. Benjamin Carson gained worldwide recognition for his part in the first successful separation of Siamese twins joined at the back of the head. Such breakthroughs aren't unusual for Ben Carson. He's been beating the odds since he was a child. Raised in inner-city Detroit, he managed, through trust in God, a relentless belief in his own capabilities, and sheer determination to go from failing grades to the top of his class at Yale and the University of Michigan Medical School ... and finally, at age thirty-three, the directorship of pediatric neurosurgery at Johns Hopkins Hospital in Baltimore, Maryland. Today, Dr. Ben Carson holds twenty honorary doctorates and is the possessor of a long string of honors and awards. *Gifted Hands* is the riveting story of one man's secret for success, tested against daunting odds and driven by an incredible mindset that dares to take risks.

Available in stores and online!

The Big Picture

Getting Perspective on What's Really Important

Ben Carson with Gregg Lewis

Dr. Ben Carson is known as the originator of ground-breaking surgical procedures, a doctor who turn impossible hopes into joyous realities. He is known as well as a compassionate humanitarian who reaches beyond corporate boardrooms to touch the lives of inner-city kids.

What drives him? *The Big Picture*. A vision of something truly worth living for, something that calls forth the best of his amazing talents, energy, and focus.

In *The Big Picture*, Dr. Carson shares with you the overarching philosophy that has shaped his life, causing him to rise from failure to far-reaching influence. This book is not about HOW to succeed—it's about WHY to succeed. It's about broadening your perspectives. It's about finding a vision for your own life that can reframe your priorities, energize your efforts, and inspire you to change the world around you.

Available in stores and online!

Think Big

Unleashing Your Potential for Excellence

Ben Carson, M.D., with Cecil Murphey

After telling the story of how he overcame an inner-city background to become a world renowned neurosurgeon in *Gifted Hands*, Dr. Ben Carson now gives an inspirational look at the philosophy of life that helped him meet life's obstacles and leap over them. Inside these pages lie the keys to recognizing the full potential of your life. You won't necessarily become a millionaire (though you might), but you will attain a life that is rewarding, significant, and more fruitful than you ever thought possible.

Available in stores and online!

Take the Risk

Learning to Identify, Choose, and Live with Acceptable Risk

Ben Carson MD, with Gregg Lewis

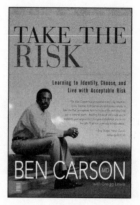

You can find our culture's obsession with avoiding risk everywhere, from multiple insurance policies to crash-tested vehicles. In our 21st-century world, we insulate ourselves with safety. We insure everything from vacations to cell phones. We go on low-cholesterol diets and buy low-risk mutual funds. But is ducking risk the most productive way for us to live? In the end, everyone faces risk. Have we so muffled our hearts and minds that we fail to reach for all that life can offer us—and all that we can offer life? Surgeon and author Dr. Ben Carson, who faces risk on a daily basis, offers an inspiring message in *Take the Risk* on how accepting risk can lead us to a higher purpose.

Available in stores and online!

CARSON SCHOLARS FUND

The Ben Carson Story

About CSF | Dr. Carson | Blog | Scholarships

The Carson Scholars Fund supports two main initiatives: **Carson Scholarships** and the **Ben Carson Reading Project**. Our scholarship program awards students who have embraced high levels of academic excellence and community service with $1,000 college scholarships. The Ben Carson Reading Project provides funding to schools to build and maintain Ben Carson Reading Rooms—warm, inviting rooms where children can discover the joy of independent leisure reading.

Through the generosity of our donors and partners, we are able to award more than 500 scholarships annually. In total, we have awarded over 4,800 scholarships across the country. Our scholars come from all across the country, and our award winners currently represent forty-five states and the District of Columbia. Carson Scholarship winners have attended more than 300 colleges and universities, and have received nearly $2 million in scholarship funds to help finance their education.

To learn more about Dr. Ben Carson and Carson Scholars Fund, visit http://carsonscholars.org/.

ZONDERVAN®
.com